# U.S. Army Uniforms of World War II

# U.S. Army Uniforms of World War II

Shelby Stanton

STACKPOLE
BOOKS

Published by
STACKPOLE BOOKS
Cameron and Kelker Streets
P.O. Box 1831
Harrisburg, PA 17105



Printed in the United States of America

First Edition

10 9 8 7 6 5 4 3 2

**Library of Congress Cataloging-in-Publication Data**

Stanton, Shelby L., 1948–
U. S. Army uniforms of World War II / Shelby Stanton. — 1st ed.
p. cm.
Includes bibliographical references and index.
ISBN 0-8117-1858-1
1. United States. Army—Uniforms—History—20th century.
2. World War, 1939–1945—Equipment and supplies. I. Title.
UC483.S624 1991
355.1'4'0973—dc20 91-13066
CIP

# Contents

# Preface

This volume, part of a series of reference books illustrating American uniform development, covers U.S. Army clothing and equipment items employed during World War II. The work focuses on the combat uniform's evolution and its utilization in battle. Selected individual and organizational equipment is also included.

Despite the number of books already written on Army uniforms of World War II, this book covers much new ground. For example, extensive research in the Quartermaster Board records provided data on the vital M1943 experimental combat uniform, as well as many components of female soldiers' field attire. Both areas were only briefly discussed in the Army's official historical studies and, despite their tremendous importance to wartime and further development of uniforms, virtually overlooked by other uniform books. Most of the photos included in this volume have never before been published.

The American military effort of the second world war was truly gargantuan, and to meet the needs of troops throughout the world, the Quartermaster Corps procured all sorts of clothing in lavish quantities. From 1940 through 1945, for instance, the Army acquired over 175 million coats and jackets, 235 million pairs of trousers, nearly 146 million pairs of boots and shoes, and hundreds of thousands of other items ranging from wet weather parkas to head toques. In order to fairly portray such diversity in this volume, a broad approach to material description and categorization was used. This differs somewhat from the method used in the first volume of this series, *U.S. Army Uniforms of the Vietnam War*, which focused on the relatively narrow subject of tropical clothing in a limited conflict.

Military uniform development is an evolutionary process. The impact of that development during World War II on the uniforms and equipment used in Vietnam can be clearly seen. The parachute jumper's suit determined design choices for the Vietnam-era combat uniform, and experimental tropical apparel directly influenced later fabric choices for a jungle environment. Appendix B (Tests of the Tropical

Uniform) details developmental work during World War II that led to clothing selections for Southeast Asian warfare.

The author wishes to give special recognition to the staff of the Natick Quartermaster Research and Engineering Center Textile, Clothing, and Footwear Division for information and developmental reports; to Dr. David Bruce Dill for his report on jungle warfare uniform development; to Cresson Kearny, Carter Rila, and John Andrews for their individual expertise; and to my editor Mary Suggs and to Ann Wagoner for their assistance in the book's production.

Shelby L. Stanton
Bethesda, Maryland
10 February 1991

# 1

# Service and Dress Uniforms

The U.S. Army uniform of World War I remained the army's military attire for many years after the war, even though the sack coat design with high-standing collar was outmoded by changing civilian fashion and not well suited for combat. The slow development of more practical clothing was only one of many effects of lack of financing for national defense, a situation that severely hampered modernization and eroded the army's fighting efficiency. The army could not afford separate uniforms for dress functions and battle conditions, so the service uniform filled both roles.

Soldiering apparel was typified by the "choker collar" service coat, worn with breeches, leggings, and marching shoes, and produced in both winter wool and summer cotton versions. The flat trench helmet and "Montana peak" service hat served as standard field headgear; the service hat was also worn for postfatigue details and drill. Minor variations in this basic uniform distinguished the different branches. For example, foot soldiers wore numerous types of puttees, wrappings, and leggings that were different, in many cases, from those worn by mounted troops. Personal equipment was limited to items adopted before the war, including M1910 haversacks, equally old intrenching shovels, meat cans, cartridge belts, and pistol or revolver belts.

Officers were distinguished by their unique Sam Browne belts, often worn with saber. The Sam Browne or Liberty style belts, holdovers from oversea campaigns and retained by officers returning to the United States, looked smart on parade grounds but identified officers, unnecessarily exposing them to enemy fire on the battlefield. The wearing of these belts became mandatory, which fortified their popularity, during Gen. John Pershing's regime as chief of staff. Field officers were also singularly visible in their high russet leather shoes with matching or pigskin leggings, field glasses, and obviously finer-quality apparel.

The service uniform remained essentially unchanged until Gen. Charles Summerall took over as chief of staff in November 1926. Within a month he declared the old uniform with its standing collar obsolete, and introduced the stylish single-breasted wool service coat with open collar and peaked lapels. He also formed mechanized and motorized forces by integrating various tank, artillery, engineer, and quartermaster elements. The mobile troops wore garrison caps, normally reserved for oversea duty, as their mark of distinction. Many items of equipment were redesigned (the haversack, for instance, became the M1928 pack assembly), but actual procurement was generally withheld because of continuing shortages of funds.

Gen. Douglas MacArthur presided over the army from 1930 until 1935 and continually called for correcting the army's materiel deficiencies as part of building a strong national defense. The Great Depression intensified the army's beleaguered financial condition. Nevertheless, certain uniform improvements were implemented. For example, in 1934 the army adopted coat-styled shirts to replace the cumbersome closed-front shirts. A year later MacArthur was succeeded as chief of staff by Gen. Malin Craig, who assumed the position as the global situation worsened. The country devoted more resources to military preparedness and General Craig took advantage of renewed congressional interest to begin rebuilding the army.

Many new items of individual equipment were designed. In 1936 new ammunition belt suspenders and pistol belts were fashioned. Mechanized personnel, whose field packs proved unwieldy inside vehicles, received handy canvas bags. Fortunately, the army's switch to the M1 rifle in 1936 did not require restructuring the cartridge belt; the eight-round clips for the new weapon fit into the belt pockets just as easily as two 1903 Springfield rifle clips.

The uniform itself began evolving in newer directions, especially after the air corps began wearing straight trousers instead of breeches. This conversion swept through the rest of the army as trousers became available, and by February 1939 trousers were designated as uniform components of all arms and service branches. The trousers were even complemented by more secure leggings, introduced in 1938.

The service uniform persisted, however, as dual-purpose clothing for both garrison and field situations. The garments did not meet requirements for a comfortable working and fighting outfit. When General Craig left office at the end of August 1939, the army still lacked a uniform with real combat utility.

# Prewar Uniforms

The U.S. Army fought World War I garbed in service uniforms adopted during 1912. The military emerged from the conflict with ample inventory, and so this uniform was retained well into the postwar era. This view of soldiers engaged in World War I training shows the steel trench helmets, cartridge belts with attached covered canteens, infantry packs, and service uniform components, including breeches with canvas leggings and marching shoes.

The "choker collar" uniform was inherently uncomfortable for soldiering, but this 1912 design remained mandatory attire for both garrison and field duty until 1926. The single-breasted wool service coat, worn here by 77th Div Distinguished Service Cross recipient Sgt. Hermann Gergresse, had four patch pockets and a standing collar fastened by hooks and eyes.

The officer's uniform was distinguished by its superior material and tailoring, and by the officer's belt, first worn during World War I and required by 1921 regulations. Various belt styles were worn—Sam Browne belts, Liberty belts, and M1921 commissioned officer's belts—but all had one shoulder strap in garrison and double shoulder straps in the field. The mounted garrison-duty attire of Coast Artillery Corps Col. John Haines (below) includes high-collared service coat with wound chevron on right sleeve and two gold lace war-service chevrons on left sleeve, dress saber chain extending from belt, riding gloves and crop, service breeches with buckskin strapping, and dress boots with spurs.

The uniform was made of either wool or cotton, depending on climate and area of service. In 1923, Major Gillespie (above) of the Ordnance Corps wears the cotton version of the 1912-pattern service coat for summer or tropical duty, along with the distinctive officer's Sam Browne belt and Pistol Expert Marksman Badge. Although the service coat with stiffened collar was a staple of immediate postwar army dress, exceptions allowed coat removal for summer or special drill fashion.

The army uniform was radically altered when the standing collar was abolished by regulations published on 31 December 1926. The new "notched lapel collar" service uniform, with its more comfortable fit and superior appearance, is displayed by chief of cavalry Maj. Gen. Guy Henry at Fort Myer, Virginia, during June 1932. Note dress boots with bright nickel-plated steel spur chains.

A military policeman demonstrating traffic signals during 1927 shows the appearance of the 1926 enlisted wool service uniform. The service hat, coat, and breeches are worn with woolen spiral leggings and shoes. The uniform was used for both garrison and field duties, and its use depended on how it was worn with other articles of equipment.

Col. William Graham, commanding the 18th Inf, wears the 1926-pattern peaked-lapel wool service coat and elastique breeches during May 1931. A plain white shirt with black cravat tied four-in-hand normally supplemented the coat when not in the field. By this time, white dress gloves were permitted at most official and social functions. Insignia of grade and distinctive insignia were worn on shoulder loops, U.S. and branch insignia on the service coat lapels.

Hawaiian Division soldiers watch preparation of poi, a food made of taro, during July 1930. The private on the right wears the uniform for tropical service in dress fashion, along with customized leggings.

Hawaiian Department soldiers marching in the 1932 Armistice Day parade wear 1926-pattern cotton service coats and breeches, along with a mixture of spiral and canvas leggings, typifying the tropical dress of the army between the wars.

Sergeant Frazier, a sharpshooter of Company F, 21st Inf, sports a full array of marksmanship badges and shooting competition decorations while stationed at Schofield Barracks, Hawaii, during April 1933.

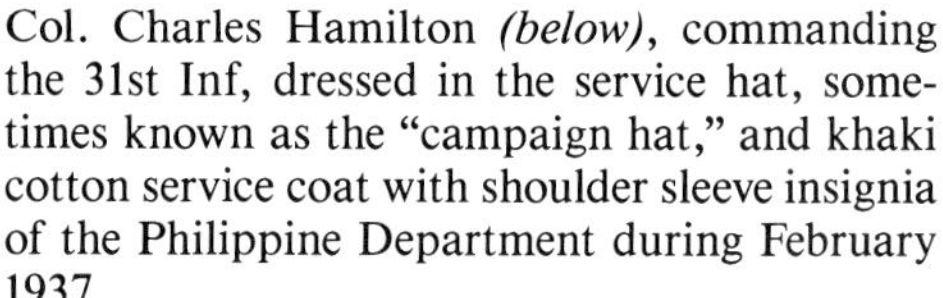

Col. Charles Hamilton *(below)*, commanding the 31st Inf, dressed in the service hat, sometimes known as the "campaign hat," and khaki cotton service coat with shoulder sleeve insignia of the Philippine Department during February 1937.

Col. Emmet Harris *(above)* of the Finance Corps dressed in the cotton khaki summer service coat with matching shirt and necktie during April 1937. The service cap had a russet leather visor and chin strap, and a band of olive-drab mohair braid.

Philippine Department signalmen wear oversea garrison dress attire, including khaki breeches and shirts with ties, during instruction on the SCR-131 radio set in April 1941. The darker-colored shirts are lightweight wool flannel, which were favored in the mountain tropics where evenings are cool. Service breeches could be replaced by trousers (which were worn without leggings) only when personnel were engaged in office-type duty indoors.

# Dress Blues and Whites

Staff Sergeant Freeman wears the enlisted full dress uniform with breast cord while in the office of the chief of cavalry during 1931. The high collar design was officially obsolete after 1926, but could still be worn if the soldier possessed full dress attire that he had acquired previously.

Army white dress uniforms endured throughout the interwar period. The white dress uniform design with standing collar, worn here by a Coast Artillery Corps major in November 1923, was abolished in 1926 and replaced by a design incorporating the lapel-collared coat.

The white mess uniform, consisting of the white mess jacket and black trousers, was worn by officers and warrant officers in the tropics but remained optional in the United States. Capt. Gaylord Fraser of the Philippine Division wears regimental distinctive insignia of the 31st Inf on his white mess jacket during July 1941.

The formal white uniform for officers and warrant officers consisted of white service coat and trousers for summer or tropical duty. Sanitary Corps Reserve Maj. Joseph Goode Jr. is dressed in the white uniform coat during 1944. Officers above the grade of captain wore two arcs of embroidered gold oak leaves on the cap visor.

Infantry Lt. Chester Hammond at a December 1939 White House reception wears the special blue evening dress uniform with shoulder knots. The braided gold aiguillette was worn on the right shoulder by aides to the President.

The 1937 regulations permitted optional special evening-wear blue dress uniforms, consisting of a dark blue mess jacket and blue cape for formal affairs. This infantry captain wears the special evening dress uniform while stationed at the U.S. Military Academy in January 1940. Note cap's chin strap, with one end forming a slide and the other fastened by a small regulation cap button at the end of the visor.

Blue dress attire was dropped after World War I but reintroduced, on an optional basis, during 1937. At that time the new blue uniform replaced the service uniform as a dress uniform. The dress blue uniform is worn by Major Gripper of the Signal Corps in July 1939; the dress blue cap has double-arc wreaths on the visor.

The *fourragère* awarded by the government of France during World War I was both an organizational and an individual decoration. The French *fourragère* was attached to the service coat's left shoulder-loop button and passed under the left arm, so that the ferret hung down in front, as worn during February 1945 by the 2d Inf Div artillery commander.

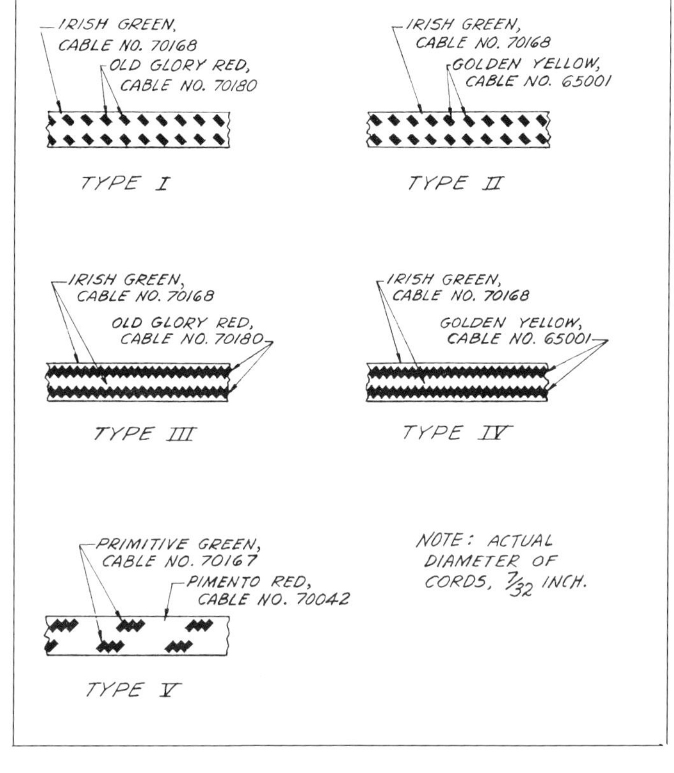


*Fourragère* decoration in rayon cord design: Type I (two citations, French, World War I); Type II (four citations, French, World War I); Type III (two citations, New French, World War II); Type IV (four citations, New French, World War II); Type V (two citations, Belgian).

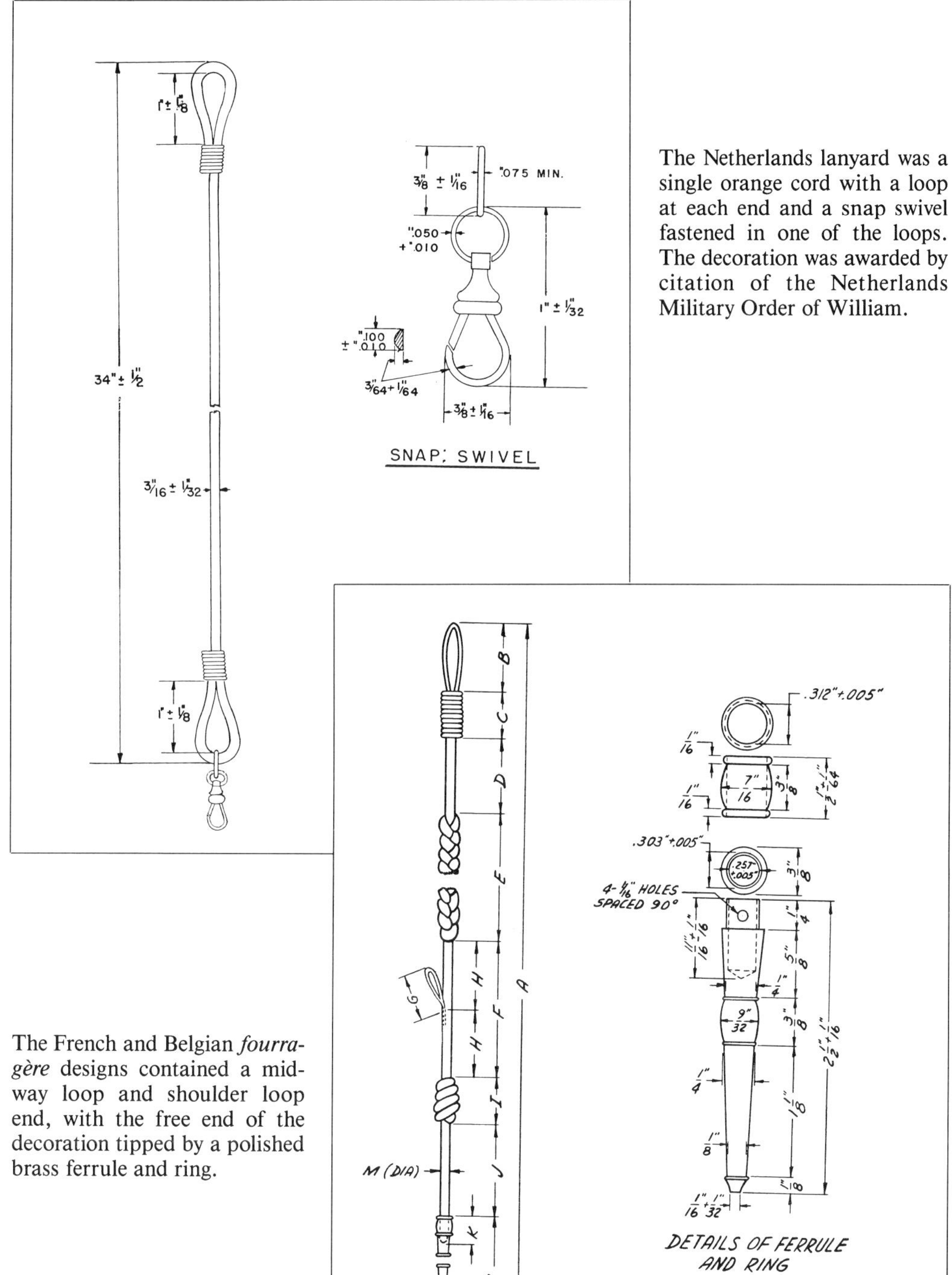


The Netherlands lanyard was a single orange cord with a loop at each end and a snap swivel fastened in one of the loops. The decoration was awarded by citation of the Netherlands Military Order of William.

The French and Belgian *fourragère* designs contained a midway loop and shoulder loop end, with the free end of the decoration tipped by a polished brass ferrule and ring.

First Corps Col. Joseph Gohn wears the 1937-pattern dress blue uniform with shoulder knots. He is decorated with the Spanish, Philippine, and China Campaign Medals, the Silver Star, the Mexican Service Medal, and the Victory Medal.

Field Artillery 1Lt. Edwin Hartshorn, aide to Brig. Gen. Dana Merrill, wears the dress blue uniform with enamel shields of an aide to brigadier general, as well as the aide's aiguillette on his left shoulder.

The dress blue coat of Judge Advocate General Captain Harbaugh, shown during July 1939. In conformity with branch coloration the shoulder straps in this case are dark blue, piped in white, and edged with gold jaceron. The four-in-hand necktie was of plain black material.

# Officer's Winter Service Uniforms

Coast Artillery School staff and faculty during the 1937–1938 session, dressed in service coats with M1921 commissioned officer's belts, service breeches, and russet leather boots closed with lacing or straps. White shirts were worn in formal dress fashion with the service uniform until August 1941.

General officer uniform with service breeches and the russet leather field boots patterned with a legging top and three buckles on the side. During 1941 two colors of officer's service breeches were prescribed; the darker shade was reserved for field use while the lighter "chino" variant became favored with the dark service coat, as worn here.

During 1942 the officer's service coat was restyled to add a cloth self-belt at the coat's waistline, fitted with a tongueless bar buckle. If he chose, the officer could add a Sam Browne belt, as shown by officers at Camp Bullis, Texas, in March 1942.

In January 1942, Brig. Gen. John Hilldring wears the officer's "pinks and greens" service uniform, a hallmark of World War II uniform apparel. By the end of 1942, officers no longer had the choice of wearing the M1921 officer's belt over the coat's cloth self-belt.

Field garrison attire of 9th Div artillery personnel during Carolina maneuvers in November 1941 includes one officer in wool shirt and trousers with leggings *(right)*, and another officer *(second from right)* wearing M1941 field jacket and khaki breeches with field boots.

Army clothing for officers and enlisted troops was deliberately styled alike, to provide a homogeneous appearance and hence battlefield protection for combat leaders. However, in spite of these intentions, the quality tailoring and superior fabric of officer's attire resulted in a sharply differing appearance. Gen. Joseph Stilwell with Generalissimo and Madame Chiang Kai-shek of China. Note officer's band of olive-drab braid on lower sleeves.

Gen. Dwight Eisenhower favored a wool jacket that could double as a battle garment and a dress tunic. He was favorably impressed with British designs, and under his direction a "United Kingdom" or "ETO-style" wool field jacket was developed. Early patterns included the Eighth Air Force ETO-style wool field jacket worn by Gen. Omar Bradley *(left)* and Eisenhower's own privately tailored jacket. Eisenhower *(second from left)* stands beside French Lt. Gen. Pierre Koenig and British Air Chief Marshal Sir Arthur Tedder.

The wool field jacket was a short, trim garment; here it is worn in combat dress fashion by 2d Arm Div officers during award ceremonies for the French Legion of Honor in March 1945. The jacket was intended for both officers and enlisted troops, but as a practical matter it was reserved for officers until after V-E Day because of unexpected shortages in 1944.

During May 1945 high-ranking officers tour Hitler's former redoubt in Berchtesgaden. They wear wool field jackets and trousers in garrison dress style for both paratrooper and nonparachutist personnel, except for XV Corps commander Lt. Gen. Haislip *(left)*, who has officer's "pink" trousers and an Eighth Air Force ETO-style wool field jacket.

The wool field jacket had a snap fastener to hold the waistband extension tab, and adjusting buckles at the side of the waistband for adjusting the fit. Gen. Mark Clark decorates an officer in occupied Austria during September 1945.

1Lt. Paul Greenhalgh of the 10th Cav wears a white commercial shirt and black cravat with the winter service uniform coat and cap during December 1934. The regimental number, when applicable, was affixed to the branch insignia.

Capt. Francis Garrecht Jr. of the 16th Field Artillery wears the winter service uniform and cap, as well as whistle cord extending to pocket, during November 1938.

W.O. Herbert Frawley, stationed at Fort Myer, Virginia, in March 1937, shows different sizes of warrant officer insignia: on his service hat and on his coat lapels.

Black cravat and khaki shirt worn with the winter service uniform coat by air corps Capt. John Godfrey. In workmanship and quality, the officer version differed considerably from enlisted coats.

Black and khaki neckties were abolished when the olive-drab shade 3 mohair necktie was prescribed in September 1942 as the only uniform tie. The olive drab also complemented the winter service uniform, as worn by Capt. Mark Gurnee of the Corps of Engineers.

Lt. Kenneth Hechler wears the lapel insignia of the Armored Center and Units, symbolized by the side view of a Mark VIII tank, with darker tan transition necktie and shirt underneath the wool service coat.

The commander of the harbor defenses of San Francisco wears the dark-shade winter shirt with khaki cotton trousers in "battle dress" style during February 1942. Regulations of 1941 dictated that the tie was to be tucked into the shirt, between the first and second buttons, whenever the coat was not worn.

Transportation Corps officer Alan Freedman wears the standard officer's winter uniform coat during December 1942. As an economy measure during wartime, wearing the collar pin with the khaki shirt was discouraged because punching a hole through the collar meant the shirt could not be used on occasions requiring informal dress attire.

The officer's winter service shirt in standard olive-drab shade 33 being worn by Maj. James Hatcher during the Carolina maneuvers in November 1941. Note numerical designation affixed to the infantry collar insignia. In August 1942 the rank was removed from the shoulder loops and replaced the right-collar "U.S." block letters.

Lt. Richard Hale, adjutant of the 110th Quartermaster Regiment at Camp Robinson, Arkansas, wears a customized officer's shirt of non-regulation pattern in dark olive-drab shade 51 during October 1941.

Air corps Capt. Charles Hall, credited by the army as the first black pilot to down a German aircraft, wears the olive-drab winter service shirt with wool trousers and garrison cap at Tuskegee Army Airfield, Alabama, during November 1944.

During April 1945 a supply liaison officer at Kunming, China, shows the overall appearance of the winter service uniform with wool shirt and trousers, garrison cap, and Blucher-pattern service shoes.

# Enlisted Winter Service Uniforms

The service coat was worn with a button-front shirt and necktie. These soldiers at Fort Leonard Wood, Missouri, during February 1942 show how the enlisted man's uniform appeared with and without the wool serge coat. Note Pfc. Solomon Bronstein *(right)* wearing 20th Inf regimental distinctive insignia below enlisted lapel discs, as prescribed by 1941 regulations.

The 1926-pattern enlisted wool service coat, worn by Signal Corps MSgt. William Groat during 1928, showing the placement of collar insignia disc on the lapels. The coat was originally designed to function as either a field or dress garment.

The enlisted wool service uniform's appearance was altered with the issuance of a newly designed coat, approved on 24 November 1939, that featured a "bi-swing" back for ease of movement. Belt hooks for a leather belt, shown here by soldiers posing with actress Hedy Lamarr, were authorized in February 1940 but deleted in March 1941 as a leather-conservation measure.

Side shoulder vents or pleat openings were part of a "bi-swing" back design introduced to enhance the field utility of the service coat. The pleats provided more fullness for ease of body movement, and are plainly visible in this soldiering publicity session at the home of actress Hedy Lamarr. The coat was made of 18-ounce olive-drab wool serge and contained a half-belt of identical material in the back.

Soldiers wearing army wool service uniform in "walking-out" dress fashion *(center)* flanked by WAC members and navy sailors. On 8 June 1942 two styling modifications were undertaken to streamline the appearance of the wool service uniform while reducing production costs. The side pleats, no longer required for field use, were eliminated because they were considered both unsightly and wasteful. The lower inside hanging pockets were altered to a double-stitched in-seam construction.

The enlisted service coat of superior quality worn here by actor Dane Clark, standing beside the daughter of Gen. Joseph Stilwell, Mrs. Ellis Cox. The cream-colored mohair necktie blended with the khaki shirt and together they presented a bland contrast to the darker service coat, rather than the previously sharp differentiation offered by the black tie.

Engineer MSgt. Jesse Gilvin performs office chores in England during February 1943. The accrued service stripes on his coat sleeve represent nearly thirty years of service.

The color guard of the 19th Bombardment Group (Heavy) wearing the service uniform in garrison-duty mode, with full decorations and color slings, after return to the United States in February 1943.

Military Police sentry at the U.S. Capitol wears the winter service uniform on MP garrison guard duty. The helmet assembly, cartridge belt, canvas leggings, and white gloves are added to the wool service attire. Further design changes in the wool service coat were incorporated in March 1943, primarily to reduce tightness across the shoulders resulting from the removal of the bi-swing pleats.

Army soldiers clad in wool service uniforms, worn with helmets and gas masks in garrison guard fashion, escort an inspection tour of Washington, D.C., antiaircraft defenses by Senator La Follette during April 1943. The wool serge coat was not suitable for combat utility because it lacked the flexibility needed for active body movement and required dry cleaning, impossible to obtain in forward areas.

Medal of Honor recipient Pfc. Lloyd Hawks, decorated for bravery while administering first aid near Anzio, Italy, during January 1944. Except for stateside garrison situations not involving field duty, service coats were kept in barracks or duffel bags. On 29 September 1944 the army formally recognized the wool service coat's diminished utility by reclassifying it to a "limited standard" basis and stopped further procurement.

Straight trousers had been adopted by the army in lieu of breeches in February 1939, although exceptions existed for troops on mounted duty or where permitted by command digression. Wool service trousers were fabricated of 18-ounce olive-drab wool serge, matching the coat material, and were worn with brown service shoes and tan cotton socks. This headquarters base section soldier at Brisbane, Australia, shows the overall fit of the wool service trousers.

During April 1941 Comanche Native Americans stationed at Fort Benning, Georgia, wear winter service uniforms in garrison dress fashion, including the M1936 pistol belt with left-side glove tab. Soldier *(right)* has the Signal Corps M1938 wire-cutter carrier and a knife.

Soldiers in occupied Germany during May 1945 are dressed in wool trousers and shirts, with and without ties, except for the individual in field sweater *(second from right).* Note privately purchased roller-bar belt fastener *(far right).*

A rare photograph of 1942-pattern Eighth Air Force ETO-style wool field jackets with first-pattern pocket flaps, being worn by enlisted troops during July 1944. General Bradley praised the heavy British wool material that served so well in both battle and dress functions. During the war, however, the Quartermaster Corps declared that similar wool fabric was unobtainable in the United States.

German Lt. Gen. Walter Hahm surrenders his command to 7th Army forces during the final battle for Germany. Many European officers considered the comparatively comfortable American shirt and trouser combination too leisurely and sometimes derided it as "golfing" clothes.

A soldier at the Fort Dix separation center turns in excess individual equipment during 1945. Discharged soldiers were permitted to retain one wool coat and a pair of wool trousers or breeches, two shirts, one pair of cotton khaki trousers or breeches, wool and khaki garrison caps, a mackinaw or overcoat (if required for warmth), one belt, one barracks bag, and all gloves, handkerchiefs, identification tags, neckties, socks, towels, underwear, and toilet articles.

Soldiers departing the army were required to have honorable discharge emblems affixed to their garments during processing and before actual separation from the service. Recently discharged Wayne Gray wears the "ruptured duck" emblem on his cotton khaki shirt in Oahu, Territory of Hawaii, at the end of September 1945.

# Summer Uniforms

Khaki-uniformed officers of the Fifth Air Force prepare to depart Eagle Farm at Brisbane, Australia, for New Guinea in February 1944. Note type A-2 summer flying jacket, center.

The tropical worsted uniform coat worn with summer service cap by Chemical Warfare Service Maj. George Gillingham during July 1944.

During February 1944 Capt. Maxwell Glenn of the 459th Fighter Squadron wears the British-inspired tropical jacket complete with embroidered insignia. This garment was unique to the China-Burma-India theater and was usually worn without a shirt.

Engineer aviation battalion commander wearing the officer's khaki cotton shirt and tie with summer garrison cap in June 1943.

The privately procured Philippine-pattern khaki officer's shirt being worn by Lieutenant Freeble of the 86th Field Artillery Bn (Philippine Scouts) at Fort Stotsenburg in the Philippine Islands during September 1941. Note officer's whistle and chain.

Lt. Monroe Franklin, shown in this May 1941 photograph, has embellished his Philippine-pattern khaki officer's shirt with embroidered U.S. and infantry collar insignia, as well as cloth bars of rank on the shoulder loops. A washable khaki-colored necktie was worn in the Philippine Department before European hostilities began, but not adopted on an armywide basis until an 8.2-ounce cotton khaki tie was introduced for the summer uniform during 1939.

The iron-creased officer's tropical worsted shirt worn by Camp Robinson commander Lt. Col. Grover Graham during July 1942.

Signal Corps Lt. Col. William Hamlin wears the cotton khaki officer's shirt with collar insignia and rank on the shoulder loops in August 1942.

XI Corps commander Maj. Gen. Charles Hall wearing the plain cotton khaki officer's shirt and trousers, a common working uniform for both field and garrison use during Pacific operations. Note roller-buckle belt fastener.

During July 1943 Maj. Robert Harrison, stationed at Assam, India, as Military Transport Service chief of administration for the Ledo Road, wears the enlisted khaki shirt with rolled-up sleeves and full shirt pockets.

Hollandia (New Guinea) Base K commander Brigadier General Wallender, left, and his cavalry executive officer wear khaki uniforms during October 1944. The officer's-pattern khaki shirt *(left)* contrasts with the enlisted-issue shirt *(right)*, with its added shoulder loops.

A lieutenant colonel of the Sixth Army wears the officer's khaki uniform with M1 steel helmet and liner, and a privately procured shoulder holster, in New Guinea during October 1944.

Philippine-pattern khaki officer's shirts worn with M1917 helmets by officers with Brig. Gen. Spencer Aiken *(left)* at the American "mud hole" headquarters during the February 1942 defense of Bataan. Officer *(right)* wears M1936 ammunition belt suspenders and pistol belt with M1918 magazine pocket.

For this January 1945 photograph, Ramgarh Training Center service commander Col. William Fuller hastily tacked a China-Burma-India headquarters shoulder sleeve insignia on his officer's khaki shirt. Locally procured uniforms regularly supplemented army stocks in locations such as Bihar Province, India.

Officers dressed in khaki garrison uniforms at Camp Joseph T. Robinson, Arkansas, during August 1942, deliver "oldest unit soldier" citation to 59-year-old Pvt. Robert Godbey *(right)*, who wears his equipment in light marching order without helmet.

During 1941 a cavalry technical sergeant, 2d Grade, wears the enlisted khaki mounted dress uniform with service hat. The 1940-pattern three-strap leather boot dispensed with lacing eyelets and hooks, which greatly facilitated putting on and taking off the boots.

The khaki cotton shirt and trousers combination was the basis for the standard army summer uniform worldwide after April 1938. The shirt, made of 8.2-ounce cotton khaki, was designed as a long-sleeved garment with two front pockets. However, the collar design mandated a tie for proper military appearance. This soldier wears the khaki uniform with cotton khaki field hat, raincoat, and M1938 dismounted leggings during 1941.

During June 1941 signalmen wear khaki summer attire with service hats at Fort Benning, Georgia. They have M1916 leggings *(left)* and M1938 leggings *(right)*. Note World War I first aid pouch at left. Under original 1937 specifications, khaki cotton trousers were somewhat tight fitting; they were later expanded in the seat and thigh to give more roominess for field utility.

The enlisted khaki uniform *(left)* worn in garrison dress fashion with garrison cap and distinctive insignia, tucked-in necktie, waist belt, and service shoes. Note the lack of suitable summer attire rendered by the "universal" M1943 experimental uniform *(right)* that relied on field trousers and suspenders worn with High Neck sweater.

The khaki field combat uniform *(left)* worn with helmet assembly, cartridge belt, protective mask carrier, and haversack, contrasted to the M1943 "universal" experimental uniform *(right)*. The test uniform for summer consisted of open High Neck sweater and field trousers with large cargo pockets. However, comparisons with the khaki uniform were actually unimportant to the field soldiers, who rarely wore khaki clothing in battle. They preferred herringbone twill fatigue clothing, which could sustain rougher combat usage.

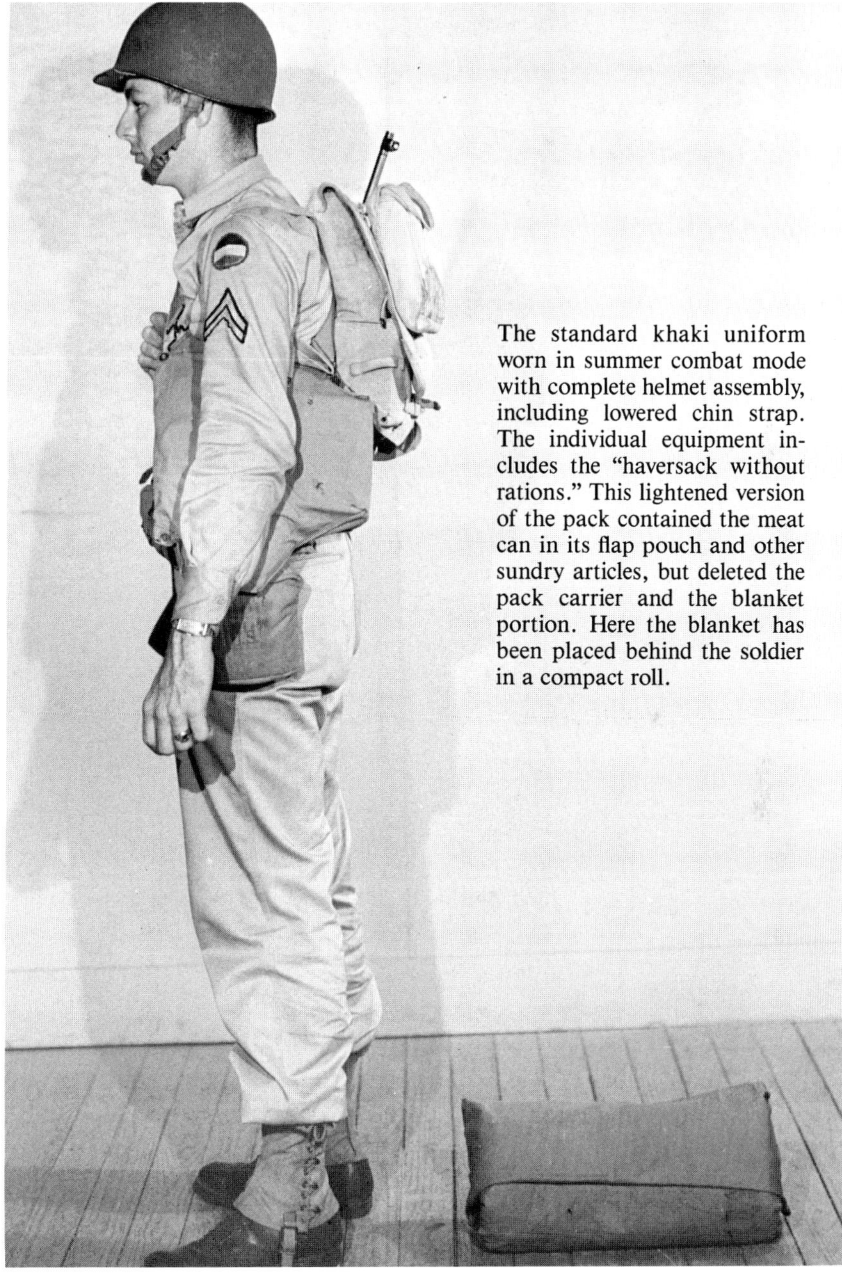

The standard khaki uniform worn in summer combat mode with complete helmet assembly, including lowered chin strap. The individual equipment includes the "haversack without rations." This lightened version of the pack contained the meat can in its flap pouch and other sundry articles, but deleted the pack carrier and the blanket portion. Here the blanket has been placed behind the soldier in a compact roll.

A 101st Coast Artillery Bn crew manning a 40mm M1 automatic antiaircraft gun at Ward's Drome near Port Moresby, New Guinea, dressed in helmets and abbreviated khaki clothing during February 1943. The army had adopted a newer shirt style with a convertible collar on 26 September 1941. This enabled soldiers to wear the shirt closed with a necktie, for garrison dress, or with the collar open for field comfort, and still present a good military appearance.

Khaki shirt and trousers worn in dress fashion with the summer garrison cap by a Technician Fourth Grade of the U.S. Army Forces, Pacific Ocean Areas. The khaki cotton trousers were made of 8.2-ounce fabric throughout the war. Expansions in seat and thigh measurements allowed greater roominess for flexibility of movement and field utility, but created a bagginess in the seat area and a less tailored appearance.

The casual working comfort of the khaki shirt is demonstrated by records clerk Pfc. Charles Gardner Jr., stationed at Myitkyina, Burma. Shortages of 8.2-ounce cotton khaki forced substitution of 6-ounce cotton fabric in shirt production for most of the war. On 24 March 1945, the army switched to 5-ounce cotton twill for khaki shirt production; it was equally durable and superior in appearance.

Corp. Lloyd Griffiths wears the khaki uniform in garrison style with open shirt, pistol belt, and field boots, as he processes through Hawaii with his records jacket.

Pvt. David Granger, former crewman on the army mine planter *Harrison* who was captured at Corregidor, wears the khaki uniform in undress fashion, with shirt pockets full, after being released from a Japanese prison camp at Kobe during September 1945.

First sergeant wears cuffed shirt and cutoff khaki trousers during medical evacuation of wounded Kachin rangers in Burma during January 1945. Instead of the recommended double-needle machines, single-needle machines were used for trouser production, an emergency wartime expedient that resulted in seams that ripped easily. The khaki uniform disintegrated rapidly in a jungle environment, and clothing shortages sometimes forced soldiers to cut down torn trousers for lack of replacement items.

During March 1944 a signal intelligence sergeant wears only a pair of truncated trousers; this extreme modification of the khaki uniform was permitted at some duty stations in remote Pacific locations.

# 2

# *Headgear*

The most distinguishing item of U.S. Army apparel during World War II was undoubtedly the popular and relatively battleworthy M1 steel helmet. It was developed as a result of widespread dissatisfaction with the M1917 helmet, a steel dishpan-style helmet hurriedly adopted during World War I for protection in European trenches. The "tin pan" M1917 helmet was functionally deficient—it offered only limited overhead protection and failed to protect the soldier from projectiles striking upward from ground level, such as exploding shrapnel.

Beginning in 1932, the Ordnance Corps began investigating an alternative design offering more coverage for the head, along with some sort of liner. As the national emergency approached in 1939, however, a satisfactory design was still pending, so the simplistic M1917 helmets were produced throughout 1940. In the following year the army adopted an entirely new and completely reshaped helmet, the M1 helmet fabricated from tough Hadfield manganese steel.

The M1 helmet assembly consisted of an outer, pot-shaped steel body and an inner plastic liner. The liner had a suspension system that could be adjusted for a snug fit for individual sizes, and it could also be worn alone for comfort in garrison situations, in areas behind the front line, or where the full helmet assembly was cumbersome or deemed unnecessary because of tropical conditions. The helmet could be used separately as a wash basin or bucket. A close-fitting wool knit cap was also adopted in 1941 to extend the helmet's usefulness in extreme cold-weather climates. More than 22 million helmet sets were delivered to the army before hostilities ended in September 1945.

The army also depended on a range of soft hats and caps. In 1939 the garrison cap was adopted as a standard item for the troops, and the "Montana peak" service hat was confined to mounted units and to departments outside the contiguous United States. A denim cap replaced the denim hat as part of the work uniform, and that hat was then redesigned in herringbone twill fabric for the herringbone twill (HBT) series of fatigue and working suits. A "sun" helmet, the cloth-covered fiber helmet, was also authorized but limited to the Philippines, Hawaii, Panama, Puerto Rico, and other tropical areas determined by the War Department.

# Helmets

The helmet was initially the shallow basin-shaped design of World War I vintage, the M1917 model here worn by a 1st Div soldier clad in herringbone twill coveralls during North Carolina training maneuvers of August 1941.

The deeper M1 helmet, manufactured of tough Hadfield manganese steel, gave more protection to the side and back of the head and was adopted in 1941 to replace the M1917 helmet. This M1 helmet assembly is worn by 37th Inf Div Technician Siravo, who destroys radio messages as a signal precaution during the New Georgia Island campaign in July 1943.

During 1941 field artillery crewmen at Fort Knox, Kentucky, fire a 75mm pack howitzer. They have "tin hat" M1917 helmets painted with Armored Force emblems: red ovals containing a black mechanized track and gun with a yellow lightning bolt.

The helmet with fastened chin straps lent a combatant appearance to dress uniforms for formation purposes, such as this decorating ceremony for personnel of the 542d Engineer Boat and Shore Regiment on Cebu Island in May 1945.

When wet, the M1 helmet had a pronounced gleam—a serious disadvantage in combat. Here 25th Inf Div commander J. Lawton Collins *(right)* confers with Maj. Charles Davis (*left*, a Medal of Honor recipient on Guadalcanal) during a tropical downpour on New Georgia Island in August 1943.

During its long tenure in army service, resourceful soldiers used the "steel pot" helmet for many functions. These 148th Inf regimental soldiers use their helmets as mixing bowls and soup buckets on New Georgia Island in August 1943.

The camouflage net was folded under the helmet's edge and secured behind the helmet liner; the elastic neoprene camouflage helmet band helped secure foliage. This photograph was part of an S-6283 information series disclosing "new military equipment" to the public.

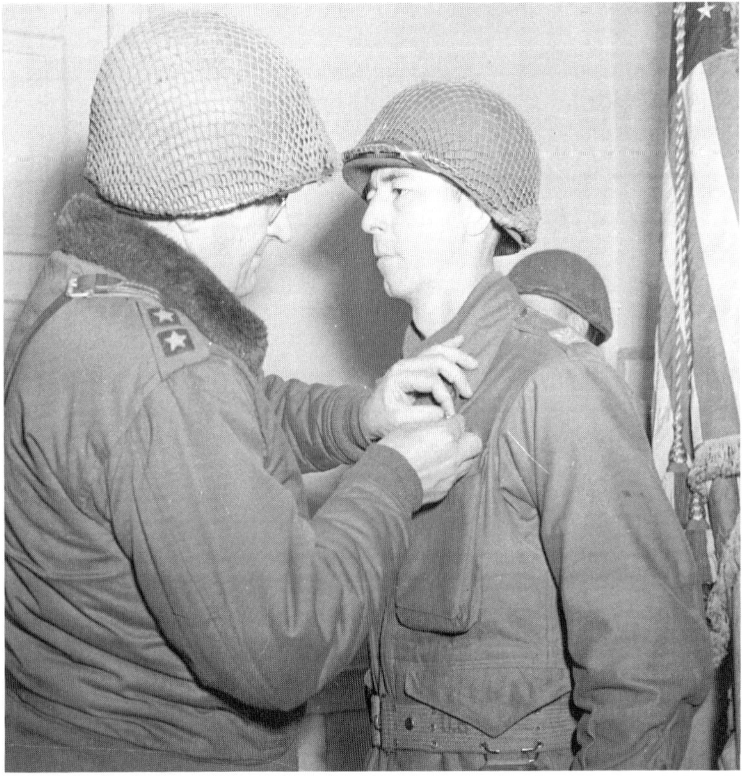

The camouflage helmet net was commonly attached without the helmet band, as shown here. Major General Eddy, wearing a modified winter combat jacket with added shoulder loops and fur collar, decorates a 4th Inf Div soldier during January 1945.

Soldiers of the 7th Inf Div advancing on Kwajalein Island in February 1944 use open netting and coral-camouflage paint to soften the helmet's glare and break the regularity of its rounded shape.

The helmet was used routinely as a pounding instrument to drive tent pins and other items, which resulted in torn netting. These 12th Arm Div soldiers are near Ansbach, Bavaria, in April 1945.

Field-expedient snow camouflage covers placed over helmets during a mechanized offensive toward the Rhine River in February 1945.

A .30 cal. Browning machine gun crew wears helmets splotch-painted for local conditions on Leyte Island, with chin straps tucked into helmet bands, in November 1944.

Divisional insignia on the helmet of Pvt. Clarence Hutchinson, 3d Provisional Reconnaissance Troop (Mounted) of the 3d Inf Div, who is taping a cracked mule hoof during Italian operations in December 1943.

A member of the 700th Military Police Border Guard Company wears a white-painted helmet liner with "MP" block letters, as well as the military police brassard, in Burma during July 1945.

Special numerical sequences were sometimes employed on combat helmets as control markings, as shown here by Lt. Kenneth Garnier after the August 1944 landings in southern France.

During the European campaign, oversized Geneva Convention markings were sometimes placed on the helmets of medical aidmen, because German forces normally abided by the rules of warfare governing front-line medics.

Sgt. Robert O'Sullivan of the 37th Inf Div wears the fiber helmet while inspecting captured Japanese ordnance in the Solomon Islands during 1943.

Army progress briefing on Bougainville in November 1943 showing fiber helmets of Admiral Halsey *(seated, center)* and Brigadier General Craig, a herringbone twill cap of Major General Beigthler *(seated, with pointer)*, and camouflage-painted helmet of 148th Inf commander Lieutenant Colonel White *(standing, center)*.

Three types of headgear worn routinely with the khaki uniform are shown in this picture: a soldier in M1 helmet *(left)* receives the Soldier's Medal from officers in fiber helmet *(center)* and garrison cap *(right)* while on New Guinea in February 1944.

# Hats, Caps, and Hoods

The officer's service cap had a russet leather visor and chin strap, and ornamentation consisting of the U.S. coat of arms, as worn by this cavalry lieutenant in May 1943. Material shortages caused the substitution of rayon for silk in hat cords.

The enlisted service cap worn by Pfc. Neal Harris at Fort Benning, Georgia, in February 1942, with Quartermaster Corps collar insignia and Infantry School distinctive insignia on the coat's lapel. Note the obviously poorer quality of enlisted-issue cloth compared to officer-grade material.

The officer's service cap worn with officer's summer uniform tropical worsted shirt and mohair necktie by Ordnance Corps Capt. Harold Glassen in August 1943.

Transportation Corps Col. John Hines wears the first-pattern garrison cap, which was constructed to form an indented top seen above the curtain juncture.

The beaten crown of a locally purchased service cap, a style normally associated with the air force's informal "fifty-mission crush" fashion, is worn here by Engineer Corps Major Gehr during construction of the Burma Road in June 1944. Note watch tied to upper buttonhole of khaki enlisted-issue shirt.

Soldiers of the 10th Inf on Iceland wear winter garrison caps with distinctive insignia during December 1941. Officers other than generals wore cord edge braiding of intermixed gold and black; enlisted troops wore the color of the arm, service, or bureau assigned.

The simpler design of the late-war "envelope style" garrison cap contained no top indentation. A captain of the 41st Arm Inf in England wears a dark green cap with a light olive-drab shirt in February 1944.

General officer's "envelope style" garrison cap, braided in gold with grade of rank insignia pinned on curtain, worn here by 4th Service Command Brigadier General Henning. He wears the serge dark shirt with dark green cap.

The khaki garrison cap complements the summer uniform coat, shirt, and tie of Transportation Corps Capt. Davis Griton in August 1943.

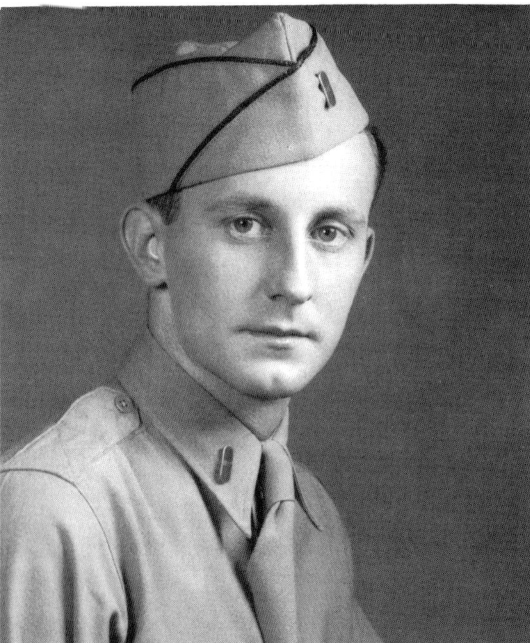

The warrant officer's garrison cap had cord edging of intermixed silver and black braid, as worn by Warrant Officer Junior Grade Grahamer of the Army Ground Forces during August 1943.

The "Montana peak" service hat with attached distinctive insignia, worn by a lieutenant of the 31st Inf stationed in the Philippine Islands in August 1941. Note locally procured Philippine-pattern khaki shirt with embroidered insignia.

The service hat for officers other than generals had a double gold and black cord with gold keeper and acorns. Note ventilation hole in crown. Lieutenant Colonel Hass wears the M1936 black necktie of silk barathea, replaced in 1941 by the black woolen worsted necktie adopted to conserve silk.

The service hat lost its Montana peak shape after prolonged field use, as shown by veterinary technologist Clarence Corliss of the Tibetan Unit of the Sino-American Horse Purchasing Bureau in May 1945.

Regimental commander Col. John Fredericks of the 129th Inf, dressed in the standard enlisted khaki uniform, wears the service hat in typical combatant style during the Luzon campaign of January 1945. The M1936 pistol belt was actually developed to be worn as shown here—supporting a sidearm holster and magazine pocket, in this instance an M1912 double-web version. Note knife sheath added to the assembly.

The herringbone twill cap with short visor was a close-fitting cotton cap, initially limited to armored troops but extended to mechanics and other specialized troops, and favored by workers like this engineer heavy-equipment operator at Lashio, Burma, in March 1945.

The SWPA khaki cap, generic to the Southwest Pacific Area, being worn with rank insignia by 31st Inf Div Brig. Gen. Thomas Hickey on Morotai Island. This was also known as the "Swing cap," because it became associated with the 11th Airborne Div of Maj. Gen. Joseph Swing.

American, British, and Chinese soldiers meet at Kyaukme in Burma at the end of March 1945. The army captain *(left)* wears the khaki uniform with the close-fitting herringbone twill cap.

The M1941 wool knit cap with its small visor extended, being worn by a cannoneer *(left)* assisting a 155mm gun crew bombarding St.-Lô in July 1944.

The M1941 wool knit cap, worn here by nurses in the field during 1944, had a reinforced visor and double fold that could be turned down to cover the ears for warmth. The nurse at left is wearing the women's trigger-finger mitten shells.

A 63d Inf Div patrol sets out at dusk to scout enemy Westwall positions during February 1945. The close-fitting wool knit cap was often favored for raiding tasks because it could be rearranged or reversed in a variety of positions to break normal soldiering silhouette.

The olive-drab cotton field cap had earflaps that could be pulled down, and replaced both the ski cap and winter combat helmet after standardization in July 1943. This photograph shows the cap being tested by the Armored Board Winter Detachment (ABWD) at Pine Camp, New York.

Colonel Gandon of the Northwest Service Command wears the pile cap with earflaps raised, while stationed at White Horse in the Yukon Territory of Canada during 1944.

During January 1945 Seventh Army Lieutenant General Patch, wearing shoe pacs with wool ski socks and an air force flight jacket, visits soldiers who wear M1943 field jacket hoods. The hoods were large enough to fit over the helmet and attach to the M1943 field jackets. Soldier at left wears leather glove shells.

The cloth hood, a less satisfactory accessory made of wind-resistant, water-repellent poplin, is worn with the M1941 field jacket by a 2d Inf Div signalman repairing downed lines in December 1944. Note the Signal Corps tool carrier.

# 3

# Combat Uniform Development and Employment

Gen. George Catlett Marshall became the army chief of staff in September 1939 and remained in that capacity for the duration of the war. He exercised strong control over the army's mobilization and performance during World War II, and his decisions and preferences in the development and procurement of clothing determined, in large part, how the army uniforms and equipage finally appeared. One of General Marshall's foremost concerns was the standardization of items to avoid needless duplication and waste of resources.

Army wartime uniform development also hinged on anticipated shortages in certain materials. For example, the early identification of copper as a scarce military commodity forced the army to seek alternatives for the brass and bronze traditionally used in everything from uniform ornamentation to eyelets, snaps, rings, end clips for webbing, and other articles of individual combat gear.

Uniform production was also affected by urgent requirements for rubber conservation. After August 1942, for instance, the heels of service shoes were manufactured with reclaimed rubber bonded to a wooden core, which eliminated the need for crude rubber in shoe construction. Even the relatively unimportant army necktie was not immune to the pressure to conserve supplies. The silk tie was replaced by a black worsted tie in 1940, and again by an olive-drab mohair tie the following year.

One of the first priorities for a practical combat uniform was the coat. A quick fix was attempted in late 1939, when pleats were added to the wool service coat to give it more flexibility for bending and reaching movements. This bi-swing design was ultimately unsuccessful, and the army followed Maj. Gen. James Parsons's mid-1940 suggestion to develop a lumbering jacket as a coat substitute. The resulting "Parsons" M1941 olive-drab field jacket was a short, hip-length combat jacket designed for both style and comfort, with two lower slash pockets and adjustable waist straps. The garment was made of tightly woven, wind-resistant, water-repellent cotton poplin lined with shirting flannel. The overlapped front closure was secured by a combination of five exposed buttons and a concealed zipper.

Once the field jacket replaced the wool service coat, the actual basis of the wool field uniform became the flannel shirt and wool serge trousers. The flannel shirting material was a wool-cotton blend with 20 percent cotton. The army considered a higher cotton content to conserve wool, but ultimately decided against it because cotton absorbed moisture and provided less warmth. The 18-ounce wool serge trousers were used extensively in the field during the first maneuver stages of the general mobilization. The tight fit of the trousers, especially in the seat, crotch, and thigh areas, caused widespread troop dissatisfaction, and the seat measurement was increased slightly in October 1941. Further pattern improvements were instituted the following year to correct other deficiencies and improve the fit. The trousers were normally worn with dismounted canvas leggings, which had completely replaced the spiral leggings during 1939.

The army quartermaster department came under increasing pressure to standardize its fighting ensemble and dispense with the multitude of outfits being developed and stocked for special-purpose troops. This coincided with the army's adoption of the layering principle, recognized by many clothing experts as superior to fur for keeping personnel warm. Several layers of loosely woven woolens trap warm air, and a light, tightly woven outer shell worn as the top layer protects the body from the wind. For the outer shell of field trousers and field jacket, the army settled on water-resistant 9-ounce sateen. By using wool and pile layers and incorporating the best features of all existing military garments, the army hoped to produce one uniform that could be worn in all temperate climates regardless of seasonal variation.

The resulting new combat uniform system developed in the fall of 1942 was designated as the M1943 experimental combat outfit. It was tested extensively in the United States and also underwent trial service in North Africa the following spring. Quartermaster Board Project T-149 was culminated in June 1943 at Camp Lee, Virginia, as the decisive field test that determined the fate of the M1943 experimental combat outfit. The newly developed items of combat equipment were tested as complete outfits and compared with regularly issued sets of standard clothing and gear. Four groups were established and were engaged in a month of intensive field exercises.

Combat Experimental Groups I and II were equipped with test items. Group I wore M1943 Model AA field jackets and Model AA field trousers and were equipped with collapsible one-quart canteens and large jungle packs. Group II had M1943 Model BB field jackets and Model CC field trousers, collapsible two-quart canteens, and small jungle packs. Both groups had ski caps, trouser suspenders, M1943 10-inch high field boots, cushion sole socks, pistol or revolver belts with .30 cal. magazine pocket cartridges, wool sleeping bags and cases, and sectional tent-ponchos. Combat Control Groups III and IV were attired in relatively standard outfits. Group III wore M1 helmet liners, prototype M1943 field coats, tan 8.2-ounce cotton shirt and trouser combinations, and they carried M1936 canvas field bags. Group IV had herringbone twill outfits consisting of working hats, jackets, and trousers, as well as synthetic resin raincoats and M1928 haversacks. Items common to both standard groups included service shoes with leggings, light wool socks, cartridge belts with M1918 aluminum canteens, web belts, shelter halves, and a wool olive-drab blanket.

During the project's trial period, soldiers walked two hours daily on the shoe test track to test field boots, cushion sole socks, and service shoes with leggings. The track contained sections of water, mud, white sea sand, logs, concrete, chipped granite, slag lava, stones, and cinders to cover a range of potential combat environments. The relative comfort of clothing and the ease of carrying equipment was judged during weekly marches on concrete roads and wooded trails. During afternoon infantry skirmishes, uniform performance could be observed as soldiers participated in patrolling, creeping, advancing by rushes, hurling hand grenades, diving into slit trenches, taking cover in undergrowth, digging foxholes, and defending against chemical attack. These exercises were alternated with obstacle courses that contained hurdles, suspension ladders, rope swings, embarkation nets, walls, and covered trenches. The soldiers also participated in bayonet and rifle drills and experimented with various cartridge belt arrangements for rapid firing and antiaircraft fire deployment. During the trial period, overall uniform practicality was also tested by engaging soldiers in routine tasks, such as pitching tents and fatigue details.

The trial period was followed by maneuvers conducted in the swampy southern portion of the Camp Lee area from 9 to 12 June 1943. The groups were divided into Blue (Experimental) and Red (Standard) forces. On the first day, the Blue Force marched eight miles toward their bivouac area before being ambushed and forced into a swamp. This opening stage gave good indications about uniform protection and camouflage properties. That evening both forces bivouacked in separate areas to conduct sleeping bag and sectional tent-poncho evaluations. That night the Blue Force attacked Red Force foot bridges in a dense swamp, allowing the value of experimental and standard combat equipment to be compared during nocturnal operations.

A torrential downpour on the second day tested the adequacy of various rainwear and packs. The poncho was judged superior to the raincoat for field use because it was easily donned, accorded fair protection from the rain, and made an excellent ground cloth. At 2 AM on the overcast second night, the Bluc Force soldiers were suddenly awakened and ordered to pack their equipment before marching eight miles to another bivouac area. The soldiers' ability to pack and carry experimental equipment items under emergency conditions was observed. A simulated battle between both forces along a corduroy road was arranged on the third day, giving a thorough skirmish test of all material. A severe late-afternoon electrical storm and rainy night dominated the last stage of maneuvers.

Both types of experimental field jackets were made of two-ply wind-resistant, water-repellent poplin that provided more warmth than cotton khaki shirts and herringbone twill jackets but were too warm when temperatures rose above 80°F. The oversized lower pockets could be filled with three hand grenades or ten clips of cartridges, but they were difficult to open when battle gear was worn because the pocket flaps were partially covered by the cartridge belt. Also, the loaded pockets struck running or crawling soldiers in the groin. A drawstring around the jacket's bottom seam could be tied in front to keep full pockets from bouncing, but this inhibited movement and made it difficult for soldiers to reach their trouser pockets.

The Model AA field jacket had a zippered back pouch to hold the sleeping bag and sectional tent-poncho. When this rear pouch was packed, however, it made the jacket tight around the neck and hampered wearing of the cartridge belt. This jacket model also contained a web belt with eyelets for attaching a canteen and first-aid kit. They were difficult to attach, however, because belt loops covered a number of eyelets. A bayonet could be attached to the web belt, but it interfered with use of the lower pockets. The jacket's distinguishing shoulder straps were ultimately judged unnecessary since they tended to snag on branches and underbrush.

The Model BB field jacket was a longer version that had an attached half-belt instead of the web belt and adjustable waist buttoned tabs, but it had no shoulder straps or rear pouch. A bi-swing back was added to allow freedom of movement, but it failed to achieve this purpose because it was improperly designed and limited to the outer ply only. The adjustable sleeve cuffs were also poorly designed and difficult to keep closed under field conditions. Nevertheless, these inconveniences were considered minor and the soldiers considered the experimental coats a great improvement over their standard M1941 field jackets.

Both experimental Model AA and experimental Model CC field trousers were made of 9-ounce wind-resistant sateen, an exceptionally tough fabric, and won favor with the troops because of their durability and their cargo pockets. There were several pocket designs. Model AA cargo pockets were double stitched while Model CC pockets had single stitching. The tendency of the cargo pockets to swing heavily when loaded with grenades or ammunition, hampering fast movement and causing leg abrasions, was reduced by shortening the cargo pockets by 2½ inches. Tight pockets that made inserting and removing objects difficult were improved with slant openings or restyled with open rear bellows at top. (See photos of cargo pocket types.) The bellows-pocket style provided the best cargo pocket configurations: Type II with two pocket buttons repositioned five inches apart and matching re-cut flap buttonholes, and Type IV with no flaps and the addition of two web straps with buckles for closure and support.

In addition to cargo pockets, Model AA field trousers had two front pockets in the waistband area. They had an inside waistband adjustment, suspender buttons, and leg-bottom adjustment tabs. Model CC versions had two front and two hip pockets, outside waistband adjusting tabs, and no lower leg adjustments. The most desirable combination was found to be one watch pocket on the right front side and two rear hip pockets. The Model CC exterior waist adjustment tab was preferred because buttons on the inside of the waistband caused skin irritation. Leg-bottom adjustment tabs also pressed uncomfortably into the leg whenever field boots or leggings were worn but were useful if service shoes were used without leggings. Suspenders and Model AA suspender buttons were required for holding up the trousers with loaded cargo pockets, since belts alone were insufficient to keep weighted trousers from pulling around the hips. However, the rear suspender buttons were initially too close together for proper support and had to be respaced seven inches apart.

The M1943 experimental combat outfit contained several good equipment ideas, but perhaps none was more appreciated than the rugged jungle pack, which was constructed of water-repellent cotton that proved capable of withstanding rough treatment in dense woods and swamp thickets. The pack's rainproof top flap had a small zippered pouch for a medical kit and other small items, and a waterproof clothing bag could fit into the main sack. The enclosing horizontal and vertical straps adjusted to accommodate pack size to varying loads, and upper and lower D-rings were used to lower or raise the pack a few inches on the back without necessitating adjustment of shoulder strap length.

The superiority of the jungle pack to the M1928 haversack was clearly established. The jungle pack rode comfortably high and its flatter and wider surface distributed the weight more evenly across the shoulders and back, while the longer and cylindrically shaped haversack exerted pressure over the narrow middle and lower back region. When soldiers were moving rapidly or fell, the relatively short jungle pack did not strike the back as hard as the unwieldy haversack.

The sack-type jungle pack allowed much easier and faster packing and unpacking, even under blackout conditions, than did the regulation haversack. The latter demanded much greater care because contents had to be prearranged prior to folding the assembly into a sack. The jungle pack offered better protection against rain and dirt, and its capacity was considerable: two blankets, one pair of service shoes, a pair of socks, a cotton undershirt and drawers, a huck towel, a set of toilet articles, six C-ration cans, the meat can, a raincoat, and one shelter half with pins, pole, and rope. The same items were extremely difficult to pack in a haversack, and service shoes had to be slung over the top. Furthermore, an overcoat could be rolled and neatly fitted under the jungle pack's flap, secured by the vertical straps. For an overcoat to be added to the haversack, it had to be placed on top of the haversack and tied loosely with the tent rope.

The experimental jungle pack's few shortcomings were minor and easily redesigned. The front and rear vertical straps were too short for proper fastening to the cartridge belt, the lower horizontal strap was too high for efficient use, the guide loops for the vertical straps were out of alignment, the drawstring slipped when knotted and prevented tight sack closure, and the attachment for fastening the shovel carrier was unsuitable when located at the top of the carrier. Redesign was delayed, however, pending comparative review with the versatile Marine Corps pack.

The experimental M1943 combat ensemble had many excellent features, but it was viewed with reservations by several branches. For example, the Signal Corps was dissatisfied with certain branch-specialized functional details peculiar to linesmen, the Chemical Corps had problems with gas-protective aspects, and the armored and airborne groups were satisfied with their existing uniforms. The highly wind-resistant two-ply poplin ski cap, with sun visor and ear flaps, was favored by soldiers over winter caps, knit caps, knit toques, and HBT working hats, but the army still discarded it because it appeared too specialized and resembled the German mountain cap.

On 16 July 1943 Project T-149 director, Quartermaster Colonel Max R. Wainer, concluded his report.

"The M1943 combat outfit, when used as a complete unit, is not satisfactory for all climates and under all conditions and cannot satisfactorily replace all of the individual items of clothing and equipment now issued the soldier in the various theaters of operations. Many of the items are satisfactory for use in a majority of the theaters of operations; others possess merit for use in limited areas. It is recommended that the M1943 combat outfit be considered unsatisfactory as an all-purpose universal set of clothing and equipment. The individual items of the outfit [should] be considered separately with regard to their suitability for use."

Although the M1943 experimental combat outfit was ultimately judged unsatisfactory for army-wide use as a complete system, many of its individual components were refined and would form the basis for several crucial standard articles. The jungle pack, for instance, became the basis of an enlarged pack that was eventually standardized as the M1944 and M1945 cargo-and-combat field pack series. Some outfit accessories, such as the collapsible canteen, were simply beyond the state of the art and had to await better plastic and molding processes. The test field jacket, however, was modified into the M1943 field jacket, and the field trouser cargo pockets were later added to herringbone twill field suits. In many respects, the M1943 experimental combat outfit was one of the most important army uniform projects of World War II.

The M1943 field jacket became the basis of the new army winter combat uniform, and completed satisfactory field testing with the 3d Infantry Division at Anzio beachhead. The outer jacket could be worn alone with wool shirt and trousers in mild or cool temperatures, and pile fabric liners could be added in colder conditions.

The army also produced a short wool jacket in response to European theater requests for something similar to the British battle dress. Production started in Britain during 1943, where it was known as the ETO field jacket, and a modified design using 18-ounce olive-drab serge was standardized on 2 November 1944 for United States manufacture. However, Gen. Dwight Eisenhower considered the wool field jacket suitable primarily as a formal garment, and his command restricted it to "noncombat wear only." This view, combined with the fact that not enough jackets were available for all ranks (thus unnecessarily differentiating officers), overrode Quartermaster General assertions that the jacket was satisfactory for field use and added a layer of warmth under the M1943 field jacket.

## European Battlefield Implementation

The experiences of the Third Army, commanded by Lt. Gen. George S. Patton Jr., provide an overview of typical clothing supply problems in the European theater of operations (ETO) during World War II. The advance component, "Group X," landed in France on 6 July 1944, but it was unable to stock enough clothing supplies. Shortly after the Third Army became operational on 1 August, the clothing situation was described as acute. The Allied advance was so rapid that supply depots could not maintain close supporting distance, and transportation priorities were reserved for gasoline and rations. By September, the Third Army's supply points were moved up as far as Chalons but the quartermaster depots were still operating merely as transfer points for ETO Communications Zone Advance Section trucking terminals and railheads. The army quartermaster stated in the September 1944 Third Army Logistics Summary Report: "The clothing and equipment situation on 1 September called for extremely urgent action. Practically no [clothing] replacements had been possible since the start of the operation. Army depots could not keep pace with the advancing Army, nor could transportation be spared for hauling this class of supplies. Practically 80 percent of issues prior to 13 September were from renovated salvage."

On 13 September 1944 the first clothing shipment of any size was delivered to the Third Army's forward depot at Verdun: thirty-eight trucks sent on a special convoy run directly from Omaha Beach. By mid-September winter clothing and equipment were given first consideration, and Communications Zone officials devised plans for transporting this apparel to the Third Army area. Unfortunately, much of the materiel was not yet on the Continent and it was already apparent that massive airlifts would have to be employed. By the end of the month improved truck service enabled most front-line division soldiers to receive their individual barracks bags, which had been stored in the rear, and most of the troops also received heavy wool overcoats.

At the beginning of October, shortages of such basic articles as overshoes, mess gear, woolen shirts and trousers, socks, and shelter halves remained critical. The status of clothing and individual equipment improved throughout the month, as more transportation was allotted, but overall supplies were still seriously low. More than 4,550 tons of winter clothing and equipment (primarily wool underwear, overshoes, sleeping bags, blankets, and ground sheets) arrived in the Third Army sector during October, most by rail, although about a quarter of the total was delivered by aircraft.

In November, the Third Army instituted heightened measures to ease the clothing and equipment shortfall. Thirteen thousand specially procured British waterproof ponchos were issued to each division as substitutes for unavailable raincoats, and the troops were pleased to discover that they provided extra warmth when used as ground sheets. Wool mufflers were also unavailable, so more than 55,000 British comfort caps were procured. An initial issue of 10,000 pairs of combat service boots was finally made to each infantry division, and armored divisions received 3,000 pairs each. After this mass distribution, combat boots were issued on a replacement basis only. All 3,000 pairs of high rubber boots were distributed to combat engineer units engaged in countering adverse flood conditions. Unfortunately, two-thirds of all soldiers in the Third Army lacked sweaters, and large numbers of front-line soldiers had neither overshoes nor field jackets.

In December the composition of the Third Army changed frequently and radically as it responded to the German Ardennes offensive. The Third Army nearly doubled in size, from nine divisions (three armored and six infantry) at the beginning of the month, to seventeen by month's end (five armored and twelve infantry or airborne), reinforced with a host of supporting assets. Clothing supply shortages went from "critical" to "extremely critical"—especially after 19 December when VIII Corps became a Third Army responsibility. The corps had lost great quantities of clothing and equipment during the Ardennes fighting, and replacing them depleted the Third Army's meager supply. The logistical problems of supply were compounded because supply stocks had been withdrawn behind the Moselle River to guard against German capture.

The most pressing problem in December was winter clothing and gear. Special winter clothing for vehicular crewmen and parka-type overcoats for other soldiers had been promised but did not arrive. All units finally received an initial issue of sweaters, but men still lacked enough canteen cups, small and medium-sized raincoats, sleeping bags, shelter halves, mufflers, overshoes, and field jackets. The large shipment of overshoes received during the month was completely consumed by the replacement of battle losses. To partially offset this problem, the Third Army quartermaster issued dubbing and impregnite to the troops. Boots and shoes could be made more water resistant if dubbing was thoroughly worked into the leather and coated with anti-gas chemical impregnite.

During December snow camouflage became a field necessity. On 27 December the 12th Army Group released 450 snow suits to the Third Army for limited "forward patrol use." The Third Army used 2,200 gallons of white paint and an equal amount of linseed oil to spray helmets, raincoats, and leggings. White cloth was not available, but the 300th Quartermaster Salvage Repair Company secured more than 5,000 mattress covers from the Reims depot and began manufacturing expedient hooded snow camouflage suits.

In January 1945 the Third Army received an average of 193 tons of clothing and equipment per day, enabling its quartermaster section to remove several longstanding shortages—such as field jackets and canteen cups—from the critical list. Shoe pacs were issued to all units, alleviating the pressing need for overshoes, but these were not supplied in large enough quantity to supply every soldier (each infantry and armored division received 6,600 and 4,000 pairs of shoe pacs, respectively). Each pair of shoe pacs was issued with two sets of insoles and two pairs of wool socks, either arctic or ski. In anticipation of calls for insole replacements, the quartermaster purchased a large quantity of felt from local markets. The January supply total also included the delivery of 700 tons of special winter clothing to the army depot at Longwy: shoe pacs, insoles, arctic and ski socks, ponchos, trigger-finger shell mittens with insert mittens, wool mufflers, cotton field caps, cotton trousers, and suspenders. On 12 January, main operations at Toul ceased and the primary clothing supply stockage was shifted to Metz.

By 21 February 1945 the Third Army was able to abandon its emergency clothing channels, and shifted to a method of requisitioning supplies on a twenty-day basis that approximated field-manual procedures. Considerable amounts of several seriously needed items arrived during the month, including enough raincoats in all sizes to fill demands. A large supply of overshoes was also received, many in the larger sizes that had been critically short. Supply levels even allowed the Third Army to halt further receipt of shoe pacs and accessories, snowshoes, creepers, and ski poles.

Within the Third Army, the 4th Armored and 26th Infantry divisions began testing different types of winter combat clothing on 10 February. The "pile jacket combination and wool field jacket uniform" (the lined M1943 field jacket with ETO-style wool field jacket) was compared to the combat winter jacket and trouser combinations. On 25 February the test concluded that the best combination was the winter combat jacket with the ETO-style wool field jacket, along with combat winter trousers and 22-ounce wool trousers. The final report recommended simplifying the combat uniform by reducing the number of composite items and it included soldiers' requests for less weight and more warmth, durability, water repellency, and wind resistance.

During March, the Third Army progressed farther in the Reich with increasing speed, and the largest problem became moving supply facilities forward fast enough to serve front-line troops. Shipments of clothing and individual equipment declined sharply because of large depot accumulations and the decreased need for winter gear. As a result, even with declining shipments, the overall list of critical shortages was further reduced. An off-loading point for clothing was located temporarily at Trier.

The clothing supply situation reverted to a highly critical stage in April, as shipments from the Communications Zone were suspended completely. Available transportation was diverted to keep the rapidly advancing units supplied with vital rations and gasoline. The suspension remained in effect until 26 April, and underwear, wool clothing, socks, and field jackets became urgently needed.

During the final campaigning month of May 1945, clothing shortages remained quite serious. Supply lines continued to lengthen, but the severely damaged German bridge and railway system prevented prompt delivery. Clothing supplies were delivered by train to the Stein railhead, where they were transferred to trucks and transported to the new Zirndorf depot. When hostilities ceased on 8 May, approximately 6,500 tons of clothing and equipment were either in the depot or on rail in the army area.

Throughout the Third Army's European campaign, reclaimed clothing and individual equipment represented an important contribution to depot stocks. A total of 3,151 tons of serviceable items was returned to use, more than 10 percent of all clothing and gear received from supply channels.

## Pacific Battlefield Implementation

Soldiers serving in the Pacific theater did not have a uniform specifically designed for tropical warfare, and the clothing provided to that theater proved inadequate. In contrast with the specialized clothing provided for extreme cold and temperate climates, the soldier in the tropics wore herringbone twill suits that were used only for fatigue duty in other regions. Cresson H. Kearny, a key army uniform development specialist, wrote vividly of his experiences in a letter to the author on 28 September 1990.

"I doubt if any of those designers have sweated nearly as heavily as I and other soldiers did while conducting jungle tests of drinking water requirements and heat stresses in Panama shortly after Pearl Harbor. During a three-day march in typical wet season humidity, those of us permitted to drink more than one quart between bivouac sites drank an average of about six quarts of water a day, but urinated only approximately one quart. Much of our sweat did not evaporate and cool us, even though our uniforms were soaked. So much sweat ran down the men's legs that those wearing essentially waterproof leather shoes were literally walking in the sweat during the afternoons. The men of the specially equipped Jungle Platoon, which I commanded, wore rubber-soled jungle boots with permeable canvas cover uppers that permitted sweat to run out from soaking-wet socks. The oral temperatures of many of us in the afternoons were around 101°F."

In the early period of jungle fighting, special attention was given to the need for protective coloration, but after trials of a camouflage pattern in both one-piece and two-piece herringbone twill garments, trousers and jackets in olive-drab shade 7 were finally adopted. In actuality, the emphasis on camouflage design diverted attention from the many other characteristics that are important in clothing worn by combatants in rain and hot temperatures. Jungle warriors not only crawled through the mud, grass, brush, and thorns of the battlefield; they were also frequently subjected to diseases and infection caused by insects and other hazards unique to the tropics.

To minimize the risk of infection from scratches and insect bites, combat soldiers kept their bodies fully covered, despite the discomfort experienced in torrid conditions. Soldiers suffered from extreme fatigue in the humid heat and complained bitterly that their clothing fit poorly and was badly designed. The troops who were engaged in island fighting found their attire hot, heavy, slow to dry, quick to get soiled, difficult to wash, and subject to snagging or tearing.

Experimental tropical uniforms were developed using alternative materials such as Byrd cloth, known to the British as Grenfell cloth. Byrd cloth was a lightweight, tightly woven herringbone twill made of long staple Egyptian cotton, and it gained eventual recognition as the finest natural material ever worn by American troops for both mosquito protection and coolness in a tropical climate. The thin, closely woven fabric shielded the soldier from mosquitoes and yet clung loosely to the skin when wet, allowing body heat to be readily dissipated through sweat evaporation. Unfortunately, Byrd cloth garments remained strictly experimental during the war.

## Development of the Experimental Tropical Uniform

In September 1943, representatives of the Military Planning Division carried out a field test in Florida, comparing poplin, Byrd cloth, herringbone twill, and Army Twill uniforms. It was found that poplin and Byrd cloth uniforms felt cooler, weighed less dry, absorbed less moisture, and dried more quickly than the HBT and 8.2-ounce Army Twill uniforms. Byrd cloth tore more readily at the seams than poplin. Against mosquitoes, Byrd cloth offered the best protection, and both poplin and 8.2-ounce twill were far superior to HBT. Taking all the factors into consideration, poplin was the first choice for uniforms. When the men were not engaged in testing, they preferred to wear poplin or Byrd cloth.

In October the Military Planning Division pointed out the advantages of Byrd cloth and poplin for jungle uniforms based on the Florida tests. Because of the shortage of Byrd cloth, the Military Planning Division recommended the immediate adoption of poplin for the jungle uniform. It was recommended that 1500 poplin uniforms be sent by air to the South Pacific for evaluation of comfort, durability, and mosquito protection.

A prospectus prepared by the QM Board, supporting the need for changing from HBT to a more comfortable and more mosquito-proof textile, was submitted to Army Ground Forces (AGF) and approved informally by them. In February and March 1944, tests under actual jungle conditions were conducted by Maj. Cresson H. Kearny in Panama. Once again Byrd cloth was found superior to HBT for coolness, comfort, quickness of drying, and mosquito protection. Adequate comparisons of Byrd cloth and poplin were not made. It was found that when wet with sweat, uniform twill trousers were too heavy and binding at the crotch.

In letters to the author on 18 January and 25 April 1990 Cresson H. Kearny, then 76, claimed that "the best and coolest hot weather uniform ever worn by Americans [was] the Byrd cloth uniform, combat proven by General Stilwell's Mars Task Force while advancing through jungle for hundreds of miles during the final campaign against the Japanese in Burma." Kearny found the uniform cool, comfortable, and mosquito resistant.

On 29 February 1944, a letter was sent from Military Planning Division to Army Service Forces (ASF) headquarters that presented all the facts then known concerning the lightweight uniform and requested a test of the proposed uniform by ground force troops in tropical theaters. AGF responded by proposing that 1000 garments be sent to each of three tropical theaters. On 15 May 1944, ASF indorsed tests for jungle combat clothing in the South Pacific, Southwest Pacific, and China-Burma-India theaters of operation by AGF technical observers and representatives of malaria survey units in those areas. ASF also stated that no action should be taken without assurance that the uniform in question could be procured in quantity without disrupting existing Army clothing and equipment manufacture. (See theater tests of tropical clothing, Appendix B.)

Early in 1944 Dr. William Mann visited the South Pacific on a special War Department mission. He wore an experimental poplin uniform and discussed its merits with experienced infantry officers and men in that theater. Their verbal indorsement was hearty and was followed by a request that experimental two-piece uniforms, 200 each poplin and uniform twill, be sent to the theater for evaluation. (See theater tests, Appendix B.)

Some who tested the poplin uniform found that the tight weave and the water repellent treatment made it hot, but it became more comfortable after repeated launderings. In tests of tropical uniforms made of poplin and of Byrd cloth at Fort Benning, however, the consensus was that both uniforms were cool and comfortable in hot, rainy weather. They also provided excellent protection against mosquitoes, unlike the HBT uniforms also worn during the test.

However, because of the favorable supply situation of the HBT trousers and jacket and in spite of the objection to the heat load and to the weight of the uniform when wet, the two-piece HBT uniform was standardized on 30 March 1944.

In June 1944 General MacArthur advised ASF against the procurement of poplin tropical uniforms and recommended, both for combat and rear areas, 8.2-ounce twill shirts with HBT trousers. He stated that poplin did not appear to be durable, was too hot, and glued to sweaty skin.

A further report from SWPA that fall stated that the HBT and khaki uniforms already in use were satisfactory and that development of the lighter weight poplin or Byrd cloth uniforms was unnecessary.

In October SWPA reported that the Grenfell cloth uniform had been tested in New Guinea for two months under rainy, humid, and hot conditions. The comparative lightness of the Grenfell cloth made it vastly more comfortable than other uniforms. "The material is considered sufficiently tough to withstand normal abusive use incidental to field service," it was reported to OQMG. The uniforms were not warm enough, however, for cool nights unless a knit shirt was worn under the jacket.

The question of the durability of the lightweight fabrics remained a concern. A wear test over a combat course was initiated at the QM Board on 20 November 1943 to determine the relative durability of poplin, Byrd cloth, and HBT (OQMG Test 1343). A preliminary report dated 28 December 1943 indicated that poplin and Byrd cloth wore about two-thirds as well as HBT. In the final report, issued on 14 April 1944, it was indicated that the rate of deterioration was greater in Byrd cloth than in poplin or HBT. The rate of deterioration of HBT was the lowest. In all cases jackets wore longer than trousers of the same material. In December 1944 the board recommended the use of 8.2-ounce Uniform Twill for trousers because it was thought to be as durable as and no hotter than HBT, it offered more mosquito protection than poplin, and it was more readily available than poplin or Byrd cloth.

In 1944 the four widely separated infantry divisions that tested the uniforms found that closely woven strong fabrics, such as Byrd cloth and poplin, were cooler than regular cotton herringbone twill material and superior in mosquito protection, durability, and cleaning properties. The excellent Byrd cloth proved too expensive for widespread adoption, but the army hoped to standardize jungle uniforms to 5-ounce poplin. The necessary facilities for its production, however, did not become available until the summer of 1945. By that stage of operations, the army was largely out of a jungle environment and moving into northern Pacific areas.

# Stateside Combat Uniform Development

The army service uniform ensemble being worn in mounted fashion by 7th Cav machine gun troops at Fort Bliss, Texas, during 1939. Note starched shirts and summer breeches with laced leather boots, and pistol lanyard on right gunner behind M1917 Browning .30 cal. heavy machine gun. Cavalry troops and several other specialized units were authorized distinctive regulation items, such as riding gloves and spurs.

During a February 1942 review at Camp Blanding, Florida, soldiers of the 26th Inf wear their winter service uniforms in "light marching order": individual equipment and helmets were added but haversacks were left unfilled. Authorization to wear trousers rather than breeches began with the air corps in 1937 and was rapidly extended to other arms and services; by February 1939 trousers with shoes became standard uniform items throughout the army.

The pot-shaped M1 helmet radically altered the soldier's appearance. Massed infantrymen wearing khaki summer service uniforms march up New York City's Fifth Avenue in light marching order with bayoneted rifles, cartridge belts, and protective mask carriers.

A common summer field outfit of Army Ground Forces was the wool uniform worn without coat or field jacket but with individual combat equipment. The ensemble is displayed by Pvt. John Tsouderos, son of the Greek premier in exile and a member of the 122d Inf Bn.

The early version M1941 field jacket with pocket flaps worn as part of the wool field uniform ensemble by the 99th Inf Bn at Camp Ripley, Minnesota, in 1943. The jacket was commonly called the Parsons jacket after 3rd Corps Area commander Maj. Gen. James Parsons, who recommended such a garment in June 1940. Note officer *(front left)* wearing long field overcoat, and Norwegian officer inspecting rifle.

The second-pattern M1941 field jacket without pocket flaps worn over the winter shirt in garrison fashion by an officer greeting Hollywood celebrities Frances Langford and Bob Hope at an Alaskan outpost. The jacket's zipper often broke and the cuffs, pocket seams, and collar frayed and soiled quickly if worn routinely under field conditions.

The advent of the field jacket during 1941 had the practical effect of supplanting the wool service coat in a field role, reverting it solely to wear around the barracks in camp and while on pass and furlough. The summer garrison uniform *(left)* was revised to include khaki garrison cap, M1941 field jacket, khaki shirt, necktie, and khaki trousers with service shoes. The M1943 experimental field jacket *(right)* was a 1942 test design that formed the eventual basis for the Parsons jacket replacement.

The M1941 field jacket was a short combat jacket that gave the winter field uniform *(left)* a new appearance. The jacket is worn here with wool shirt and trousers, leggings, Type II service shoes, and individual battle gear, including a 1923-pattern dismounted cartridge belt. The M1943 experimental uniform *(right)* and equipment articles are exhibited as worn during combat trials in North Africa.

The standard winter field uniform ensemble *(left)* with Parsons M1941 field jacket and individual battle gear, including revised M1910 haversack and pack with "quick-push" buckles on strap around shelter half. The new buckle design permitted soldiers to loosen or adjust straps quickly while wearing mittens, a great improvement over the original buckles that often jammed in cold or wet weather. The M1943 experimental uniform *(right)* with prototype field pack is exhibited as worn during combat trials in North Africa.

The Parsons M1941 field jacket was made of windproof and water-repellent cotton poplin with a flannel lining. Although several design improvements were made during 1941, the jacket did not wear well and lacked sufficient toughness for use as a combatant outer shell. It is photographed supplementing the winter garrison attire of Colonel Glandon at the headquarters for the Alaska Highway in Yukon Territory during 1944.

The 1940-pattern blue denim work clothing with hat, used by an engineer testing land mines at Fort Belvoir, Virginia.

The 1940-pattern blue denim work clothing worn on fatigue duty. The trousers were styled like the khaki trousers and contained both side and watch pockets.

The early-pattern one-piece herringbone twill work suit, with two breast pockets and inside-hung patch hip pockets, worn with heavy leather gloves in this June 1941 photograph. This garment was intended for mechanics as well as personnel of the Armored Forces.

The first two-piece herringbone twill work suit, distinguished by its jacket with two center-pleated pockets and bottom band finish, worn in June 1941 with matching hat.

A squad of the 30th Inf, clad primarily in blue denim garments with service hats, prepares a new 37mm antitank gun for service at Presidio of San Francisco during October 1940.

The 1941-pattern herringbone twill working outfit and the army's 1938-style blue denim fatigues modeled by quartermaster personnel during November 1941. Neckties were unauthorized with work clothing and reveal the posed nature of this quartermaster photograph.

Standard work uniform *(left)*, worn here in typical field utility fashion, consisted of the early-pattern herringbone twill jacket, with pleated breast pockets, and trousers worn with hat. The M1943 experimental uniform *(right)* field jacket and trousers are shown in similar field utility mode.

The 1941-pattern herringbone twill jacket and trousers *(left)*, worn in field combat fashion with individual battle gear, also constituted the usual summer training mode for Army Ground Forces. The M1943 experimental uniform *(right)* is exhibited as worn during combat trials in North Africa.

The metallic buttons used on herringbone twill clothing, shown on the jacket of M4 tank gunner Corp. Raymond Borucki from the 191st Tank Bn.

When laundered, the herringbone material faded from dark olive-drab to a light sage green. On left is the first-pattern jacket with pleated pockets and trousers with inside-hung pockets; the version on the right has later-style jacket and trouser "bag pockets" adopted for ease of manufacture.

The stark contrast between unwashed herringbone twill field clothing *(left)* and washed outfit *(right)*, showing the fading that negated camouflage advantages. The trousers of the crawling infantryman on the right are clearly visible, even though he is moving across a field of dead winter grass.

M1940 experimental suits of printed cotton and rayon camouflage design being tested by the Engineer Board at Fort Belvoir, Virginia, during 1941.

Engineer camouflage testing at Fort Belvoir, Virginia, during 1940 included individual "chicken wire" nets draped over the soldier and sprinkled with natural foliage.

The 1940-pattern experimental camouflage suit was similar to the German parachute smock pattern but the styling resembled early-model Soviet camouflage coveralls. Seasonal coloration variety was planned.

Engineer Board 1940 tests at Fort Belvoir, Virginia, demonstrate the difference between camouflaged trooper *(left)* and soldier ordinarily dressed in wool combat uniform *(right)*. Note how the plain helmet allows ample detection of both troops.

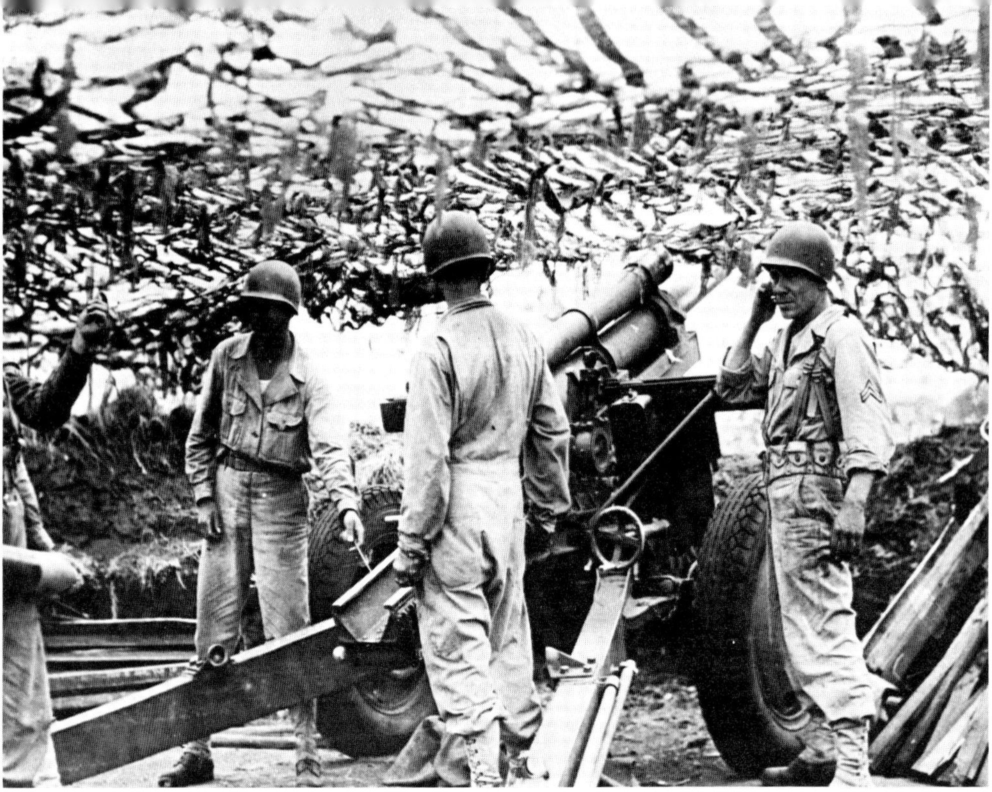

Summer combat clothing employed by artillerymen in a firing position, protected by camouflage netting. The one-piece cotton herringbone twill suit is worn in center, while soldier on right has his herringbone twill jacket tucked into trousers.

A camouflaged herringbone twill suit, apparently painted in ad hoc fashion, being displayed for publicity purposes at the Los Angeles opening of the 1943 movie hit *This Is the Army.* The soldier is flanked by young actor Capt. Ronald Reagan and wife, actress Jane Wyman.

War rescue dogs and their handlers exercise in Alaska. The soldiers have winter field uniforms, and their equipage includes M1928 haversacks and gas-mask carriers. The dogs are outfitted to transport emergency ration packs.

The slipover, High Neck buttoned wool sweater was produced for cold areas as part of the field outfit assembly. The prototype model is shown in this picture, along with M1943 experimental trousers and suspenders, during Quartermaster Board testing.

# M1943 Experimental Combat Outfit

The M1943 experimental combat outfit was a set of battle clothing and equipment tested by the Quartermaster Board from November 1942 until July 1943 for possible worldwide application. It represented the army's desire for a universal combat ensemble for all purposes. Components are displayed during trials at Camp Lee, Virginia: *(Left to right)* standard cotton khaki uniform and standard herringbone twill uniform used for comparison purposes; test outfit with AA model field jacket and AA model field trousers; test outfit consisting of BB model field jacket and CC model field trousers.

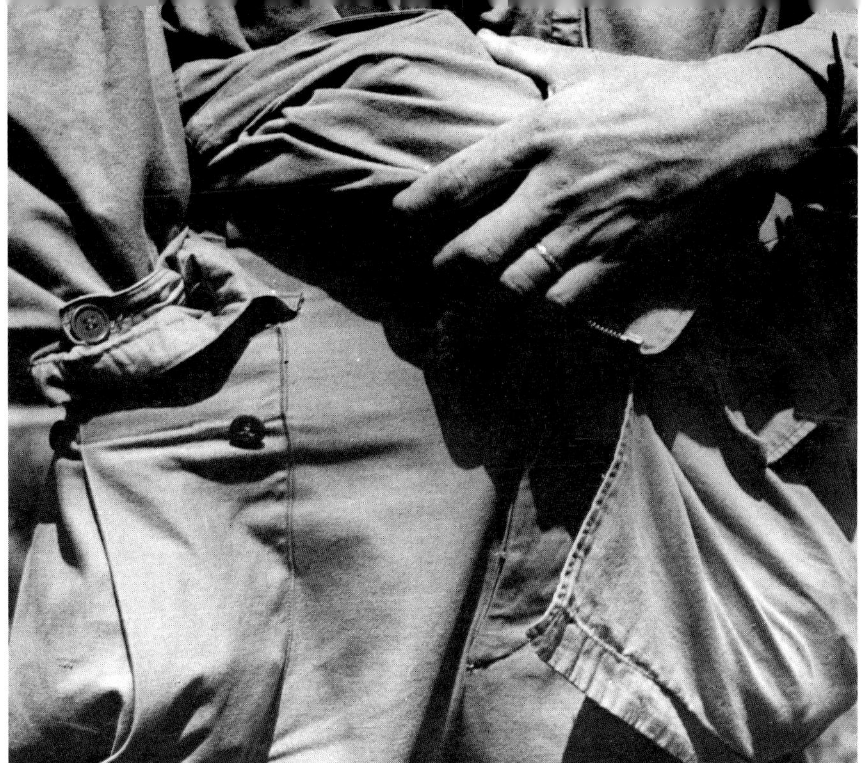

The lower pockets of the M1943 experimental field jacket swung heavily when fully loaded, hitting the groin of soldiers engaged in combatant activity. Access to trouser pockets was inhibited if jacket pockets were full, mandating use of both hands to retrieve extra grenades in trousers.

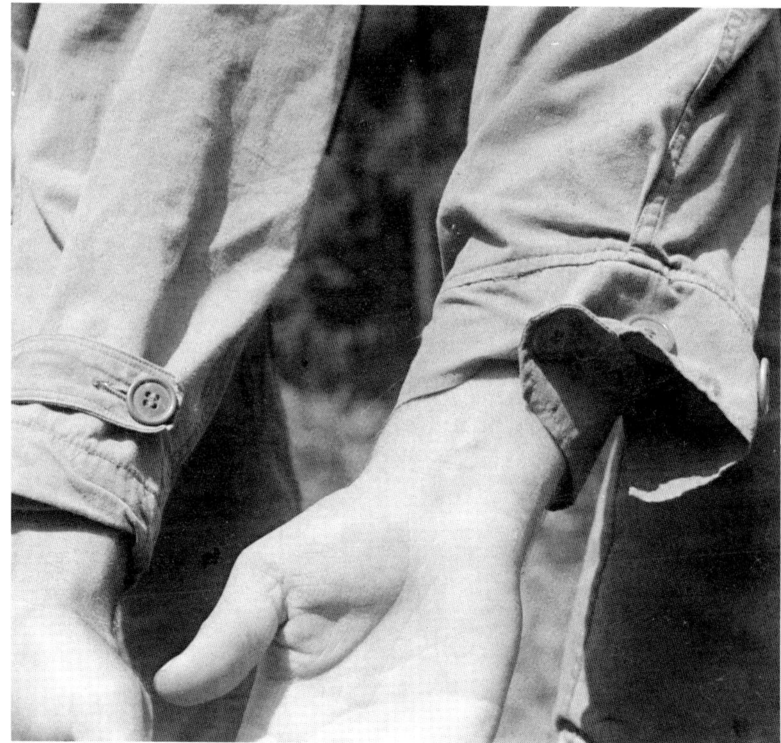

The wrist-strap closure of the AA model *(left)* was preferable to the BB button arrangement *(right)*, which came undone when soldiers were crawling under test conditions.

1

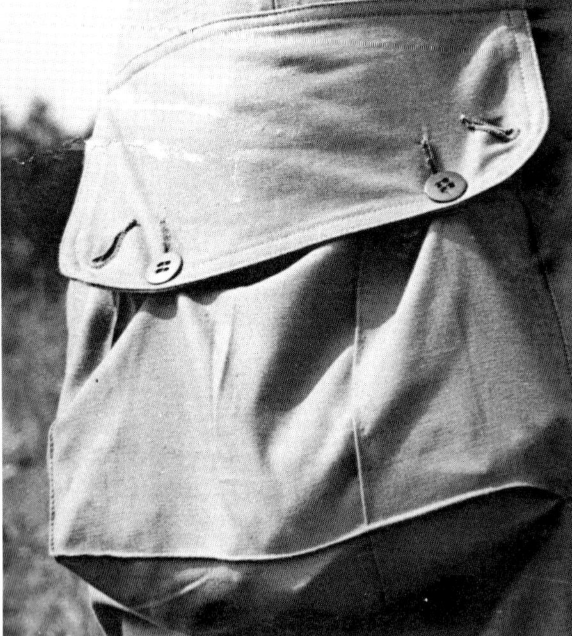

2

The five types of cargo pockets of the experimental M1943 field trousers, shown loaded with three grenades each, during Quartermaster Board testing at Camp Lee, Virginia.

1. Type I slanted cargo pocket with flap closure.
2. Type II bellows pocket with two additional buttonholes added to flap and buttons reset five inches apart.
3. Type III open bellows pocket with two 9-ounce sateen tabs and buttons for closure and support.
4. Type IV open bellows pocket with two web straps and buckles for closure and support.
5. Type V open bellows pocket with snap closures.
6. Unmodified combat pocket design of the field trousers.

3

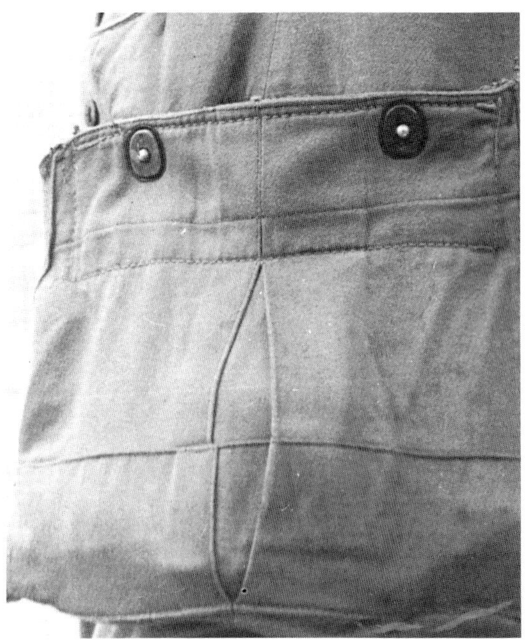
5

4

6

The outside waist strap of the M1943 experimental field trouser CC model *(left)* was preferred to the AA model's inside strap *(right)*, which bulged at the waist and pressed the button uncomfortably against the body.

Suspenders carried the weight of loaded trouser pockets far better than a belt. Test trousers at left had one pocket reconfigured into a type IV design, while trousers on right contain modified type III combat pockets with support straps extending from the watch pockets.

The unmodified trouser cargo pockets swung far forward when loaded with objects such as grenades.

The goal of the experimental M1943 combat outfit was to incorporate the best clothing features and items of specialized branches into one optimum set of clothing and equipment. Here the strong influence of parachutist clothing and gear is apparent. However, note the difficulty of access to the trouser cargo pockets.

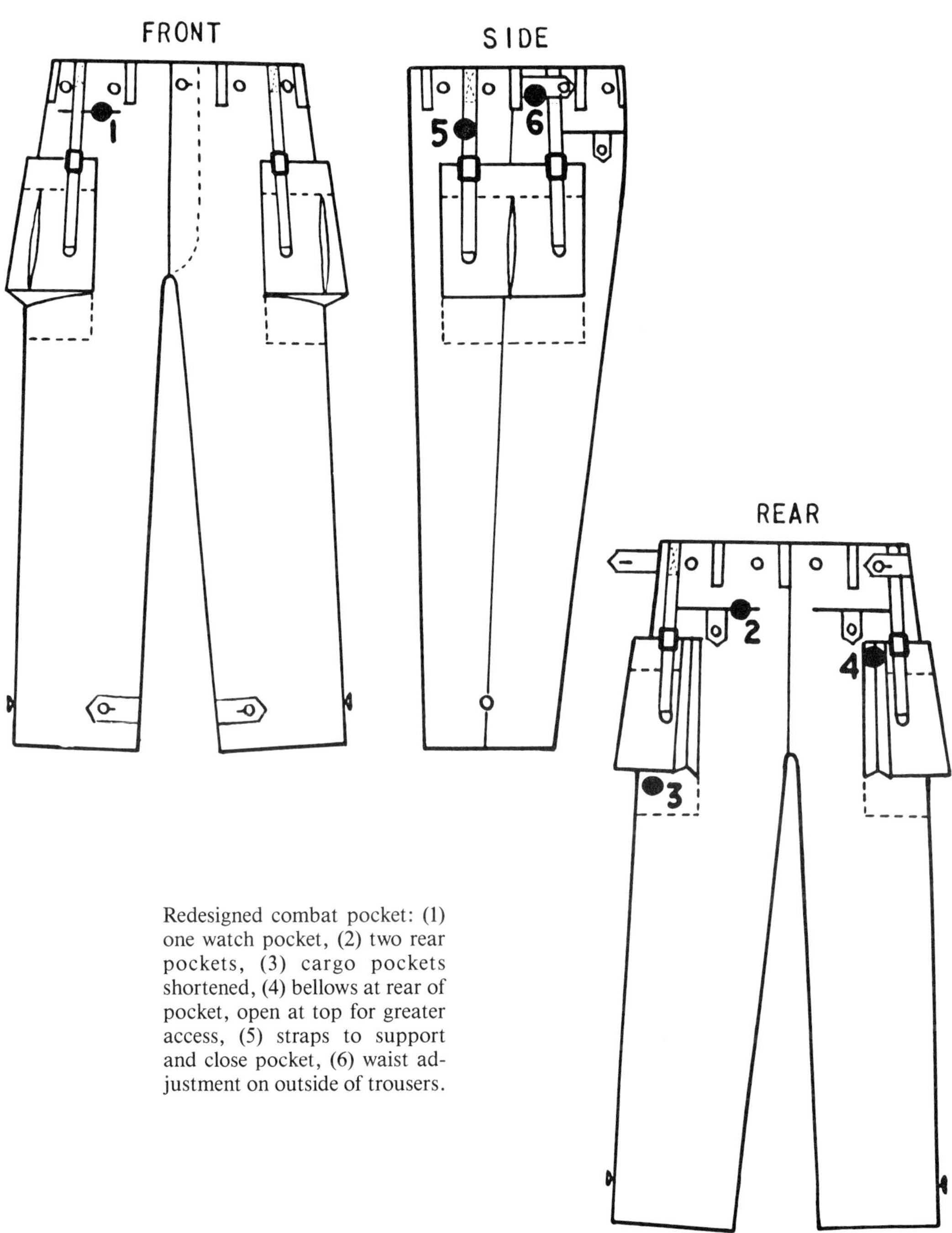


Redesigned combat pocket: (1) one watch pocket, (2) two rear pockets, (3) cargo pockets shortened, (4) bellows at rear of pocket, open at top for greater access, (5) straps to support and close pocket, (6) waist adjustment on outside of trousers.

The original M1 magazine cartridge pockets had back loops for inserting the pistol belt, but removal of the pistol belt caused the pockets to fall off. Holding the belt at the other end caused pockets to slip over the fastener.

*(Photo at right)* The arrangement of duck M1 magazine cartridge pockets, designed to carry two clips of ammunition for either M1 rifle or carbine, often overcrowded the pistol belt. Note how top belt has ample space with two pockets, a canteen, and first aid packet pouch. The second belt's four pockets allow sufficient space for attaching pack straps, but reduce accessibility to rear pockets. The third arrangement's five pockets equaled ammunition capacity of the M1923 cartridge belt, but impeded belt fastening. Six pockets at bottom made equipment attachment extremely difficult.

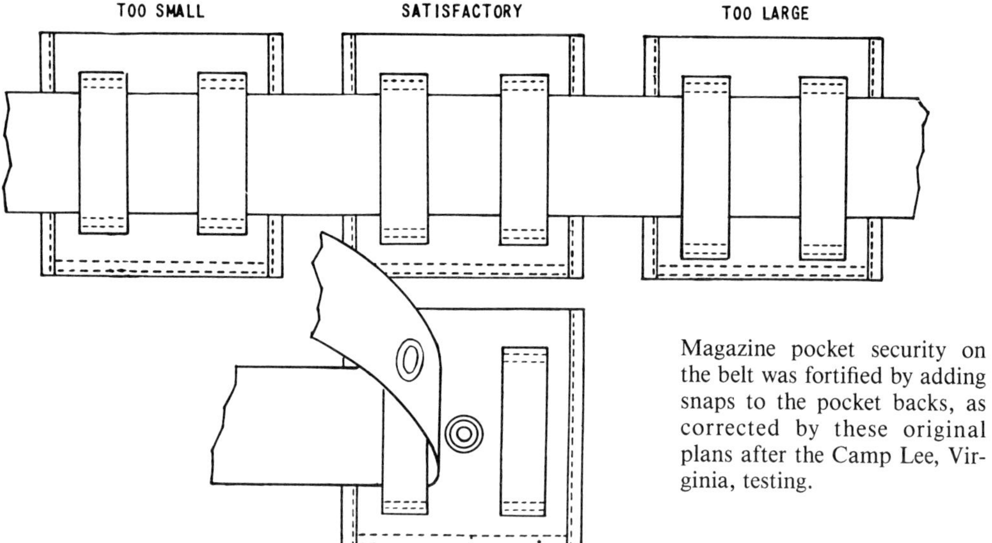


Magazine pocket security on the belt was fortified by adding snaps to the pocket backs, as corrected by these original plans after the Camp Lee, Virginia, testing.

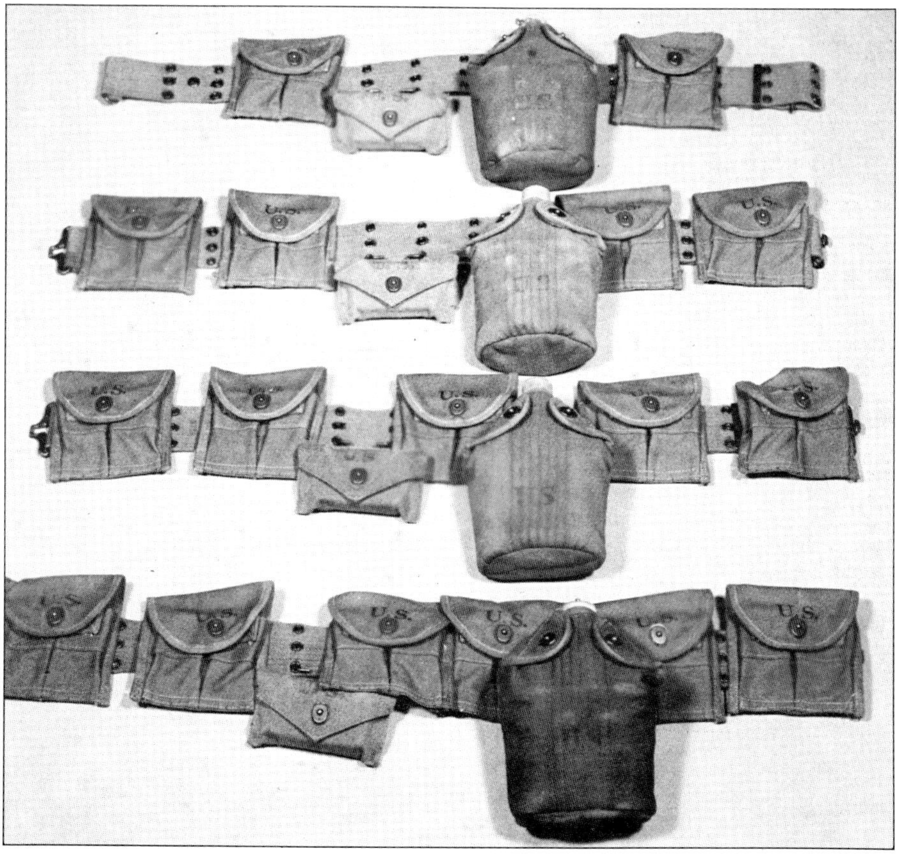

The location of the shovel-carrier fastening hooks on the grommets of the jungle pack: type A carrier top hooks *(right)* proved unsatisfactory because they allowed the shovel handle to hang below the bottom of the pack; type B shovel carrier with hooks at the base, or open end of the carrier *(left)*, kept the handle even with pack bottom. Note how the jungle pack's horizontal and vertical straps could be adjusted to accommodate varying loads while keeping the pack compact.

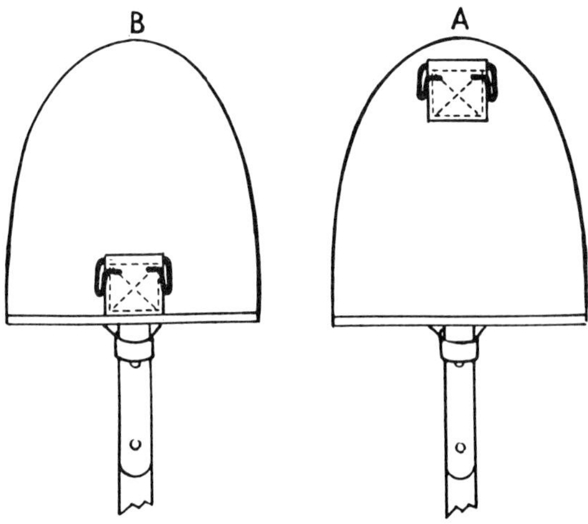

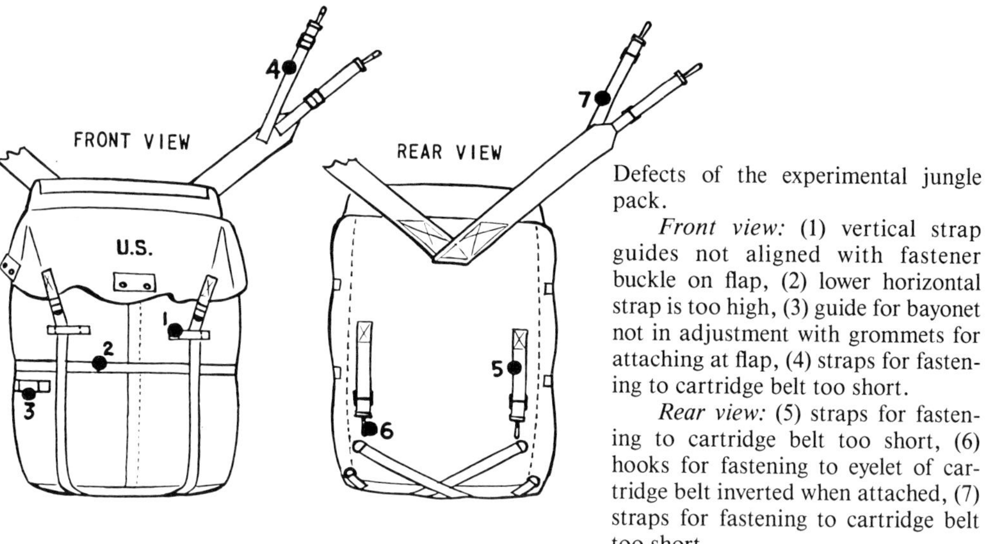


Defects of the experimental jungle pack.

*Front view:* (1) vertical strap guides not aligned with fastener buckle on flap, (2) lower horizontal strap is too high, (3) guide for bayonet not in adjustment with grommets for attaching at flap, (4) straps for fastening to cartridge belt too short.

*Rear view:* (5) straps for fastening to cartridge belt too short, (6) hooks for fastening to eyelet of cartridge belt inverted when attached, (7) straps for fastening to cartridge belt too short.

The jungle pack's experimental drawstring arrangement *(left)* at the sack opening slipped when tied. A more effective closure *(right)* was secured by lacing the cord through the grommets, beginning with the first grommet to the left of the center seam and ending with the cord passing through the same grommet a second time. After the string ends were tied together, the sack closure was drawn tightly, secured with a slip knot, and covered with the pack's rainproof flap.

The haversacks—actually canvas wrappers into which equipment was rolled—were unsatisfactory for use in the tropics because they were tedious to assemble. A soldier operating in a rain forest or swamp was often unable to spread out the cloth or arrange his articles in an orderly fashion. In addition, the full haversack's long, narrow, and cylindrical shape hampered movement in confined, vine-tangled jungle and exerted pressure down the middle of the wearer's back, as indicated by the shaded area in illustration.

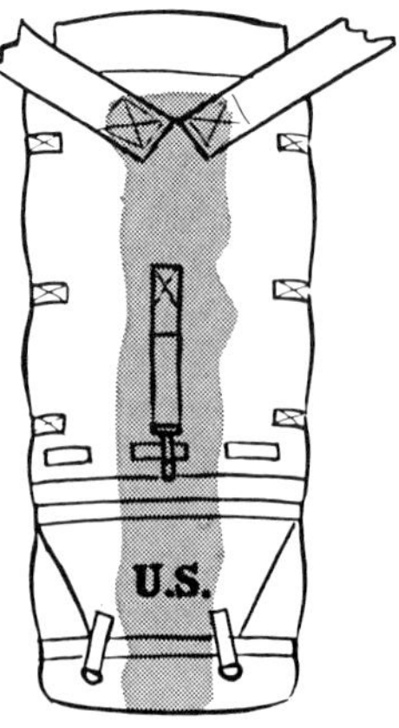

The jungle pack evolved from work initiated by Capt. Cresson H. Kearny in Panama; it was basically a canvas sack containing a rubberized waterproof bag to keep its contents dry. The enclosing straps ran horizontally and vertically so that the pack could be readily adjusted to any size; the top flap had a small zippered pouch for sundry articles. The jungle pack was also shorter, wider, and flatter than the haversack, and distributed pressure more evenly over the back and shoulders, as noted by the shaded area in illustration.

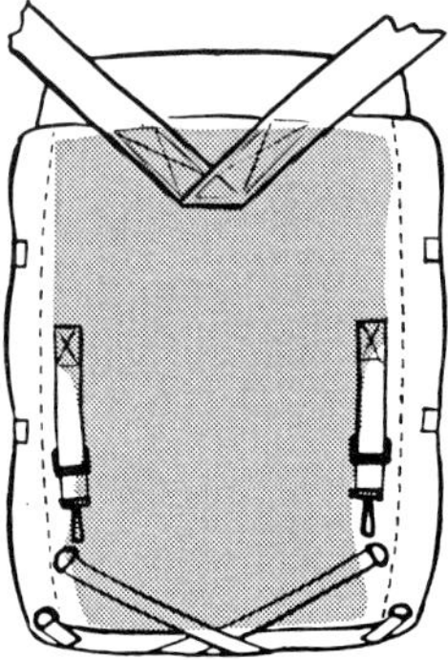

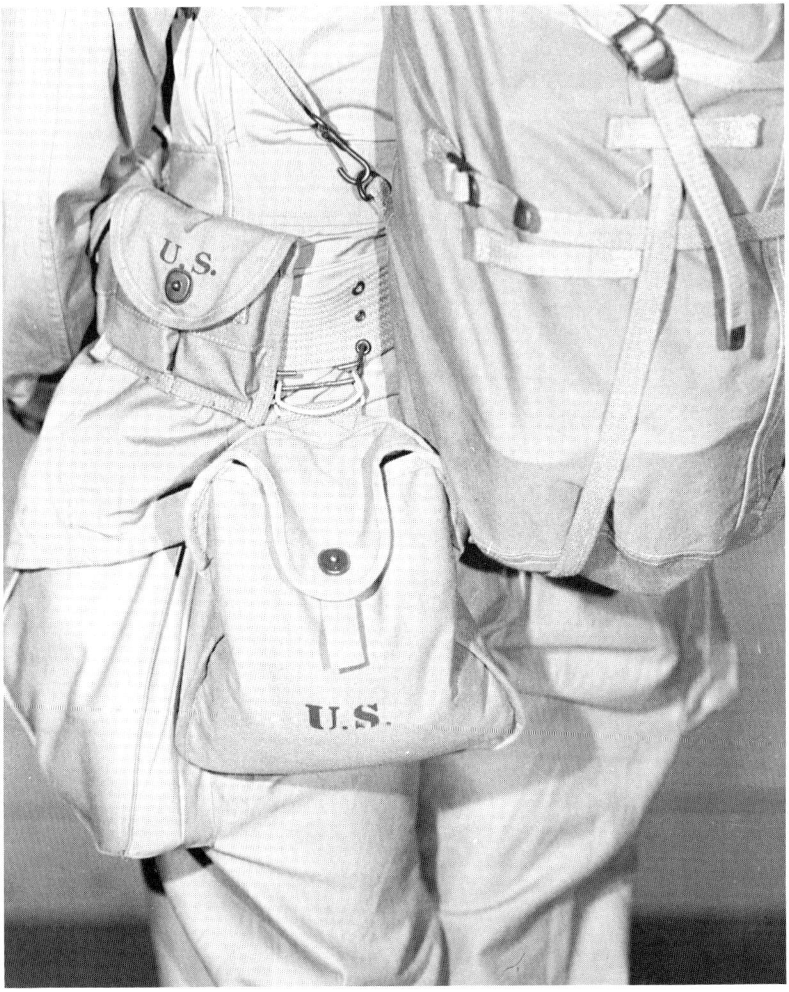

The two-quart experimental collapsible canteen was more comfortable to carry than the standard canteen and practically noiseless, but its manner of fastening onto another hook linked to the pistol belt was unsatisfactory. The canteen often came loose when pushed upward by contact with the ground or by striking some object.

The collapsible canteen attachment clip, as seen in photo insert, started to disengage from the hook on this soldier's pistol belt as he sat down and the canteen was pushed upward. The canteen slipped off completely when the man stood up.

M1943 experimental combat uniform outfit.

1. Tent, poncho, sectional
2. Pack, jungle
3. Suspenders, trouser
4. Bag, sleeping, wool
5. Trousers, field, M1943
6. Belt, pistol/revolver (pistol belt shown with cartridge, magazine, .30 cal.)
7. Canteen, collapsible
8. Case, sleeping bag
9. Sweater, High Neck
10. Cap, ski, prototype
11. Cap, field, variant
12. Socks, cushion sole
13. Coat, field, M1943
14. Boots, field, M1943, 10-inch
15. Overcoat, field, liner
16. Overcoat, field, M1943

Front view of the M1943 experimental combat uniform.

Side view of the M1943 experimental combat uniform.

Rear view of the M1943 experimental combat uniform with prototype jungle pack.

# Combat Attire, Europe

Winter service uniform worn in "combatant dress" fashion during the change of command for the 1st Inf Div in August 1943. Major General Huebner *(left)* wears enlisted-issue shirt with shoulder straps added. Maj. Gen. Terry Allen *(right)* wears enlisted shirt with nonregulation shoes and gaiters. An early-pattern engineer compass case is hooked to his pistol belt.

Standard garrison attire in Europe consisted of the winter shirt with wool trousers, worn here by 34th Inf Div Distinguished Service Cross recipient Lt. Edwin Frey in Italy during September 1944. Note officer's shirt with shoulder straps and helmet liner with rank superimposed over painted division insignia.

The flannel shirt worn with trousers as formal attire by a lieutenant receiving the Distinguished Service Cross at Ingolstadt, Germany, from Lt. Gen. George Patton Jr., who is wearing the wool field jacket and special general officer's belt with general's issue sidearm modified by personalized grips.

During July 1944 in Normandy, France, a 9th Inf Div medical aidman wears the special flannel shirt, modified to permit a front flap and sleeve gussets, with the Geneva Convention brassard.

During November 1944 a 104th Inf Div infantryman garbed in "light combat order" fires his M1 Garand .30 cal. rifle near Weisweiler in the Rhineland. He wears the M1912 cartridge belt, M1910 aluminum canteen, blanket roll tied over M1943 field jacket, a folded raincoat, and a shovel protruding from underneath the bedding roll.

Forward soldier of a patrol advancing toward Aachen in the Rhineland during September 1944 is dressed in herringbone twill coveralls with leggings. He is armed with a .45 cal. Thompson submachine gun, while others carry carbines.

Troops of the 29th Inf Div advance toward Brest, France, in September 1944. Soldier at left wears ammunition bandolier over an M1941 field jacket worn inside out (with dark lining contrasting with lighter cloth), and is followed by soldier in M1943 field jacket equipped with magazine belt for a Browning automatic rifle. Front soldier at right has ammunition carrying bag.

In April 1945, 42d Inf Div troops push into Wuerzburg, Bavaria. Soldier with 2.36-inch M18 rocket launcher is equipped with ammunition carrying bag and a rolled-up wool sleeping bag.

Wounded soldier placed on inflated M26 life preserver on Omaha Beach during the D-Day invasion. The medical aidman holding plasma infusion bottle *(left rear)* has the rubber gas-mask carrier, and the captain *(center)* wears a winter combat jacket. Soldier kneeling at right is equipped with M1936 field bag suspenders. The invading troops were lightly equipped because additional items, such as shelter halves, were carried in blanket rolls on the vehicles of following units.

During November 1944 a carbine-armed military policeman *(left)* directs traffic in Nancy, France. Both soldiers wear Parsons M1941 field jackets, and the military policeman has second-pattern dismounted canvas leggings. Note the sign giving distance to New York City *(upper left)*.

Maj. Gen. J. Lawton Collins decorates a 1st Inf Div soldier in France during September 1944. The soldier is wearing the M1941 field jacket with pistol belt and early-period M1912 magazine pocket. The coat suffered from excessive fraying along the collar roll and sleeve cuffs, and its outer buttons snagged in belts and equipage. As a result, as early as mid-1943, the once-promising field jacket was regarded as lacking enough warmth and durability for sustained combat wear.

The M1941 field jacket was often conspicuous because of its color: a lighter shade than the darker olive-drab of the winter wool uniform, as evidenced by this 3d Inf Div soldier guarding German prisoners in Italy during 1944. He carries the lightweight protective mask carrier.

*(Above)* During December 1944 a 104th Inf Div soldier wears the M1943 field jacket over an M1941 field jacket with upturned collar, revealing the tab fastener for closing the collar around the neck. Note the gusset construction of the M1943 field jacket sleeve.

*(Below)* The M1943 field jacket's inside drawstring allowed adjustment for better fit. The jacket was intended for normal temperate winter climate, with layering added for arctic, cold-temperate, or mountainous areas. The Mediterranean coastal plain was chosen for its initial combat test, and the jacket was standardized after 1,567 garments received high praise from the 30th Infantry's 2d Bn at Anzio during March–April 1944.

*(Left)* The M1943 field jacket was considered an improvement over the Parsons M1941 field jacket in appearance, camouflage, and utility. The stylish design is shown by 101st A/B Div Brig. Gen. Gerald Higgins, who wears the field jacket with green-backed combat leadership tab underneath star during April 1945.

Fifth Army Lt. Gen. Mark W. Clark *(right)* decorates a 91st Inf Div soldier in November 1944. Both are wearing M1943 field jackets. General Clark was instrumental in securing standardization of the jacket, noting that the most important feature of the Anzio test was his troops' discovery that they could fight out of their jacket pockets. Note that General Clark's raised lower pocket flap also reveals the inside pocket strap with its concealed buttonhole tab.

In contrast to General Clark's acceptance, the ETO command regarded the M1943 field jacket unsightly and defective. General Bradley noted that the combat soldier slept in his overcoat, and the jacket was useless for leg warmth. The European theater refused to accept the jackets, except in minimal amounts, until fall of 1944. Here 79th Inf Div soldiers wearing M1943 field jackets relax after an October 1944 battle. Upper cargo pockets gave ample storage room, and the normally concealed button (*left*, exposed by tucked-in flap on Pvt. Arthur Muth's jacket) prevented snapping while moving past underbrush or ground obstacles. Sgt. Kelly LaSalle *(right)* has M3 trench knife and lensatic compass carrier.

In April 1945, XV Corps military police dressed in winter garrison-style mode wear M1943 field jackets while guarding a headquarters in Haar, Germany. Many commanders disliked the garment's loose fit for this kind of formal guard function. Guard at left wears carbine magazine pockets.

A sergeant trudging through mud near St.-Dié, France, wears the M1943 field jacket with herringbone twill field trousers, overshoes, and rubberized assault pack during November 1944. The cotton field trousers were normally worn over 18-ounce wool serge trousers.

Mortar crew of the 79th Inf Div, wearing two-piece cotton herringbone twill suits of the later-pattern "box pocket" style, moves forward in France during July 1944. The soldiers are equipped with mortar carrying pads slung around their shoulders.

Infantrymen of the 79th Inf Div push through Mirecourt, France, during September 1944, wearing combat field packs over their M1941 field jackets. Soldier climbing ladder has full pack while soldier at right has haversack empty of bed roll. Both carry M1943 shovels.

A paratrooper *(left)* watches a mortar crew of the 36th Inf Div in full equipment, including gas-mask carriers and general-purpose waterproof bags strapped over field packs, march toward Cisterna, Italy, during May 1944. Rear soldier has additional gunny sack for rations, while soldier in front of him carries an extra ammunition bag, and center soldier transporting mortar rounds has a mortar sight case.

Assault troops of the 3d Inf Div board LST vessels for the invasion of southern France during 1944, their helmets embellished with "playing card" identifications. The soldiers wear haversacks devoid of bedding, and the individual at rear of first column is equipped with the medical bag.

These 85th Inf Div troops rotate into front-line positions under smokescreen protection in Italy during February 1945. They wear M1943 field packs, which were made available by simply redesignating the jungle pack as a general pack. They also carry a mix of M1910 intrenching shovels *(second from right)* and M1943 intrenching shovels.

First-pattern "Trapper Nelson" or "Yukon" packboards with canvas and wooden frames used to bring supplies forward to positions of the 91st Inf Div in Italy during September 1944. Packboards were considered organizational rather than individual equipment.

A machine gun crew trails a column of the 63d Inf Div approaching Eschringen, Germany, in "light marching order." The soldier on left carries a pack frame with field chests.

Soldiers of the 4th Inf Div gazing at overhead Allied aircraft in the vicinity of St.-Lô, France, during July 1944 wear herringbone twill jacket and trouser outfits. Center soldier has hand grenade in pocket of cartridge belt, M1923 intrenching shovel and carrier, and lightweight gas-mask carrier.

Cannoneers of an 8-inch howitzer in Italy during January 1944 are dressed in different field attire. The front rammer is wearing cotton field trousers, the center artillerymen have herringbone twill trousers, and the soldier bending at right is dressed in wool trousers.

A machine gun crew firing in September 1944 displays the two primary trouser types worn in European combat. The soldier with M1938 wire-cutter carrier *(left)* wears 18-ounce wool trousers, while machine gunner *(center)* has the cotton field trousers that could be worn over them in colder weather. Under winter conditions, however, even 20-ounce wool test trousers proved inadequate, leading to recommendations for napped 22-ounce wool trousers.

Rifle squad of the 3d Ranger Infantry Bn in the Santa Maria sector of Italy during November 1943, equipped with light gas masks slung over their M1928 haversacks. Ranger *(left)* also has M1910 pick mattock and carrier.

Troops of the 10th Mtn Div wear mountain jackets while fighting in Italy during March 1945. The hooded mountain jacket was windproof and water-repellent and featured a large cargo pocket extending across the back. The soldier at right also carries a BAR ammunition belt and canteen.

During January 1945 soldiers of the 75th Inf Div march toward the Colmar front carrying M1943 field packs. These items were simply reclassified jungle packs, but the Quartermaster Corps held standardization in abeyance until combat results were known, and made only limited procurement during the war. The troops are being passed by an 18-ton M4 high-speed tractor hauling logs.

These infantrymen engaged in hedgerow fighting near Canisy, France, during July 1944 were soon forced to discard their new camouflage suits because of the close resemblance to German camouflaged garments.

The army's failure to provide initial snow camouflage or adequate winter clothing to its troops at the onset of the 1944–45 winter campaigning season in Europe is graphically demonstrated by this machine gun team of the 90th Inf Div, giving covering fire to troops—equally conspicuous in dark olive-drab uniforms—counterattacking toward the Bastogne–Wiltz road in early January 1945.

When snow began to fall during December 1944, the lack of winter camouflage material forced quick field-expedient solutions—such as snow suits made from mattress covers. These 1st Inf Div troops counterattack through Belgium in January 1945.

# Combat Attire, Pacific

During March 1944 on Bougainville Brig. Gen. William Arnold *(left)* and XIV Corps commander Maj. Gen. Griswold *(left center)* wear herringbone twill jackets, with second-pattern "box pocket" styling, while decorating a 37th Inf Div officer *(right center)*, who is dressed in a 1941-pattern two-piece herringbone twill suit with pleated pockets. Soldier *(center background)* has a one-piece herringbone twill mechanic's suit.

The standard one-piece herringbone twill suit displayed by 98th Inf Div Lt. Col. Hagan during Hawaiian training in 1945. Soldiers disliked the garment because it had no drop flap and disrobing was required when relieving the bowels. The pistol or cartridge belt array with suspenders further hampered garment removal in the field.

Troops of the 37th Inf Div on New Georgia during August 1943 have two-piece herringbone twill field outfits; standing soldier *(left)* has a one-piece herringbone twill suit and rubber boots. The two-piece work suit was preferred because it allowed more air circulation and enabled the soldier to perform bodily functions without undressing completely.

During May 1944 an army photographer, engaged in covering the New Guinea campaign, is shown wearing the two-piece herringbone twill work suit with pleated pockets. The neck closure is secured and sleeves rolled down for mosquito protection. Note the M1923 dismounted cartridge belt, with pointed flaps and "U.S." markings prominently stenciled on the right front cartridge belt pocket.

During February 1944 an army combat photographer, attired in the two-piece herringbone twill field suit, records the battle for New Britain. Note trousers' bag pockets. Herringbone twill suits were usually worn in the field because they withstood the rough jungle terrain better than cotton khaki, and their greenish color offered better camouflage.

A patrol from the 43d Inf Div crosses a stream during the Munda campaign in July 1943, dressed in herringbone twill jackets buttoned to the neck for protection against insects and jungle debris. The lead soldier with an M1 Garand rifle is followed by a soldier carrying a 1903 Springfield rifle, favored for use as a grenade launcher.

A navy Seabee, attired in the early-style one-piece herringbone twill work suit with M1928 haversack, poses in the Pacific theater before combat deployment during April 1943. Except for the sailor's white hat, the clothing and equipment are standard army field composition. Note details of the inside-hung side pockets and watch pocket.

During 1944 quartermaster combat clothing tests in New Guinea, the soldier standing *(left)* in an amphibious tractor shows obvious perspiration through the loosely woven herringbone twill fabric. The poplin material on soldier to his right proved cooler, lighter, and quicker to dry—despite the tight-fitting M7 shoulder holster strap—and more protective against mosquitoes.

A soldier of the 96th Inf Div fighting on Okinawa during May 1945 wears the herringbone twill jacket with individual equipment: an M1923 dismounted cartridge belt, jungle first aid pack, canteen cover, and wrist compass. The suits of troops moving into forward areas were often dyed darker green for camouflage purposes, but olive-drab shade 7 was selected by the time of the Okinawa battle.

Soldiers of the 37th Inf Div, clad in two-piece herringbone twill suits, give supporting fire in the battle for Manila during February 1945. The picture highlights the differences between third-pattern "bag pocket" herringbone twill trousers *(far right)* and second-pattern "box pocket" herringbone twill trousers *(second from right)*.

Members of the 1st Cav Div pose in the Admiralties during June 1944. Most of those standing wear khaki shirts mixed with herringbone twill trousers. The dark coloration of the twill fabric reveals recent issue; after one or two washings, the material faded noticeably. The two-piece herringbone twill suits are third-pattern garments with bag pockets; trooper kneeling in left foreground has coveralls.

Artillerymen move the trail of their medium howitzer during a September 1943 fire mission on Arundel Island, while clad primarily in cutoff early-pattern herringbone twill trousers with inside-hung pockets.

Howitzer crew of the 192d Field Artillery Bn during the 1943 Solomon Islands campaign wears truncated 1941-pattern herringbone twill trousers.

Command post of the 86th Antiaircraft Artillery Group on Saipan manned by personnel in khaki and herringbone twill clothing. Soldier in center wears a Marine-issue undershirt.

Troops of the 43d Inf Div land on New Georgia during July 1943 wearing mixed gear: M1910 haversacks with buttoned meat-can pouches *(foreground)*, an M1928 haversack *(center foreground)*, and jungle packs. Some soldiers have neatly compacted packs, others have looser bedding rolls.

Soldiers garbed in standard herringbone twill field clothing huddle from enemy fire immediately after landing on Leyte in the Philippine Islands during October 1944. The infantryman beside the wire spool *(left)* has a machine gun cleaning kit behind his machete, while his comrade *(right)* carries a camouflaged jungle pack.

Soldiers of the 96th Inf Div advance on Leyte Island during October 1944. The Browning automatic rifleman *(left)* has M1928 haversack and an ammunition bandolier, soldier *(center)* carries a general-purpose ammunition bag in addition to his M1928 haversack, and kneeling soldier *(right)* is equipped with M1936 canvas field bag and jungle medical kit.

Troops of the 1st Cav Div cross a water-filled tank trap on Leyte Island during October 1944, wearing M1910 intrenching shovels and machetes on their jungle packs. Note the gleaming leather binocular case, a symbol of leadership which made a good target for enemy snipers.

*(Below)* During July 1945 a soldier advances on Okinawa wearing an M1937 magazine belt for the Browning automatic rifle, two stainless steel canteens, and the first aid packet pouch hooked underneath the jungle first aid kit.

*(Left)* The one-piece jungle suit, known as the frog-skin suit, was camouflaged with reversible outer green and inside tan patterns, so that the garment could be worn either normally for rain-forest conditions or turned inside out for combat on beaches or rocky territory. Here 37th Inf Div Pfc. William Stewart examines a Japanese .25 cal. sniper rifle on New Georgia.

Signal linesman SSgt. Gardner Burns wears the camouflaged "frog-skin" jungle suit while using a climbing belt and safety strap to string communications wire on New Georgia Island during August 1943. The troops reported that the suits were too heavy, hot, and uncomfortable for tropical conditions.

Infantrymen of the 37th Inf Div wear one-piece jungle suits during the Solomons campaign. The suit's internal fabric suspenders permitted raising or lowering the crotch to prevent chafing, and the cargo pockets provided convenient storage space for hand grenades and other items.

Soldier attired in the one-piece jungle "frog-skin suit" *(right)* helps to mount a .50 cal. machine gun onto an ex-Japanese barge in New Guinea during May 1943. He is assisted by a soldier *(left)* dressed in 1941-pattern herringbone twill jacket with the buttoned bottom band. Two-piece camouflaged jungle apparel was adopted after troops continued to complain about the lack of a drop seat in the coveralls-style garment. Note jungle packs on deck.

Trooper of the 124th Cav regiment in Burma wears Quartermaster General T-309B poplin tropical jungle clothing with water-repellent treatment while leading a pack mule. Both poplin and Byrd cloth were cooler, weighed less when dry, and dried quicker than other fabrics tested. The tightly woven fabrics also gave superior mosquito protection. Unfortunately, wartime demands hindered production of this type of clothing by diverting 5-ounce poplin to the manufacture of other military articles.

Quartermaster Technicians Fourth Grade at Assam, India, wear British-style tropical jacket *(left)* and one-piece herringbone work suit *(right)* during August 1945.

Lt. Gen. Joseph W. Stilwell wears the service "campaign" hat and M1941 field jacket, showing the adjustable strap at hip line, in northern Burma during March 1944.

Using a 75mm pack howitzer as a map table during the northern Burma campaign in November 1944, Maj. Raymond Schultz in herringbone twill jacket *(left)* confers with Chinese Major Wang, who wears pullover sweater normally worn underneath the service coat. Soldier *(right)* wears the "jungle" knit shirt.

Troops of the 5307th Composite Unit (Provisional), known as *Merrill's Marauders*, move toward the front in Burma during February 1944. Left soldier wears the herringbone twill "sad sack" hat, along with M1928 haversack with folded raincoat stuck loosely in straps. The pack animals are outfitted with Phillips cavalry pack saddles.

Troops of *Merrill's Marauders* rest along a mountain trail. The soldier in left foreground has an M1928 haversack with M1910 intrenching shovel and medical kit bag.

War dog handlers of the 5307th Composite Unit cross a Burmese river during 1944, wearing field jackets *(left and right)*, herringbone twill combat jacket *(middle)*, and jungle packs. Note towels on pack straps and dog *(left)* with medical pouch.

While leaving Assam, India, Lt. Gen. Joseph Stilwell wears a Chinese army cap, M1941 field jacket, and early-pattern M1938 dismounted canvas leggings. This view shows the arrangement of two lace eyelets per hook, a complexity dropped after brass supplies became critical.

Army liaison personnel assigned to the Chinese Training Center during 1944 wear Chinese winter uniforms complete with Republic of China cap emblems. Rank tags worn above left breast pockets signify officer status (yellow for colonel, blue for captain, and so on) while the lack of tag indicated enlisted or interpreter positions.

# 4

# Wet-Weather and Cold-Weather Clothing

With the onset of the national emergency just prior to U.S. entry into World War II, the army began seeking a satisfactory substitute for the rubberized raincoat that had been standardized during 1938. Various resin-based coatings were investigated, including the expensive Goodrich Company synthetic named Koroseal. After considerable developmental work, field testing began in 1942, but by summer the adverse rubber situation demanded the immediate adoption of synthetic resin.

Because of manufacturing expense and technical delays, the Quartermaster Corps had to adopt two different types of raincoats: double-coated raincoats with stronger seams and coats made of single-coated fabric with cemented seals. In all cases, the wartime army raincoat was a straight-front coat with five buttons, two open-through pockets, and no hood. Rain suits and lightweight ponchos for tropical areas were designed in nylon.

At the beginning of World War II, the army's double-breasted overcoat, made of 32-ounce olive-drab melton wool, represented a revised pattern. The overcoat was initially considered an integral part of the soldier's winter combat outfit, but the introduction of field jackets and layered trouser combinations relegated the overcoat to garrison situations or excess baggage. However, the severity of the European 1944–45 winter and shortages of proper arctic garments forced the army to reverse this policy. Under these circumstances, the overcoat was temporarily issued as an emergency item of warmth for front-line combatants.

The development of new cold-climate and mountain apparel stemmed from dissatisfaction with the prewar Eskimo-influenced "Alaskan clothing." A new line of arctic apparel was field tested and evaluated by special ski and snowshoe patrols in the northern United States during the winter of 1940–41. These trials proved that furs and other dense materials could be replaced by loosely woven inner garments layered under windbreaker outer shells. Such layered clothing retained warm air while still promoting ventilation, which allowed perspiration to evaporate. After the trials, fur and shearling (or yearling lambskin) were replaced with pile clothing, made of alpaca and mohair, beneath windproof shells.

The first pile parka overcoats combined the pile with the outer shell. Later the pile was converted into a separable liner that could be removed or added depending on temperature—a considerable improvement. The two-layer poplin shell itself was reversible and could be worn with either white or olive-drab coloration exposed to cover more terrain situations. The final two-part composition design gave better coverage to a wider range of climatic conditions and proved much easier to clean and maintain. An arctic field jacket with heavier lining and greater length was also developed, designed for wear in conjunction with the high-necked sweater and muffler.

Hoods and gloves were also a vital part of any winterized outfits. Wool inserts were developed for wear inside specially designed mitten shells, constructed of tough wind-resistant 9-ounce sateen, which had enlarged gauntlets secured with wrist straps and a trigger finger that was placed away from the palm on the backside so it would not interfere with normal functions. A range of caps and hoods was also developed, including a detachable hood especially fabricated for the M1943 field jacket to give the soldier overall head and neck protection from the elements.

Accessories such as skis and snowshoes also underwent revision during the war. The army adopted an ash- or red oak–framed trail snowshoe based on the narrow Indian or "Cook Inlet" design, with its characteristic upturned toe. An emergency snowshoe, of less satisfactory but more easily stored elliptical design, was provided for personnel who would need such specialized footwear for only short periods—such as snow-stranded drivers. Various types of sleds and toboggans were given improved harnesses that made them adaptable to hauling by either men or dogs.

# Wet-Weather Apparel

Rubber was eliminated from raincoat manufacture within a few months after the United States entered World War II and was replaced by oil-treated fabrics and synthetic resins. These soldiers of the 452d Antiaircraft Artillery Automatic Weapons Bn, with a towed M1 40mm antiaircraft gun, wear raincoats in France during November 1944.

An 88th Inf Div military policeman, wearing raincoat and helmet with MP lettering, checks a Dodge three-quarter-ton 4 X 4 truck on the northern Italian front during January 1945. Note collar upturned to protect the nape of the neck, necessitated by lack of a raincoat hood. This is a first-pattern raincoat without sleeve straps.

A company commander's runner within the 2d Inf Div, attired in raincoat with sleeve strap loops and buckle, uses the hand-held SCR-536 radio at Koenigsfeld, Germany, during March 1945. Note carbine outfitted with M8 grenade launcher.

Pvt. Charles Preston of the 5th Inf Div wears the raincoat under winter conditions as he brushes snow from his jeep-mounted .30 cal. Browning machine gun in Luxembourg during December 1944. The wool knit cap with field-expedient ear flaps is worn under the helmet.

Raincoats being worn by infantrymen passing through Schirmeck in Alsace during November 1944, showing the early storm-shield back design.

Combat engineers guard the Roer River in February 1945; they wear three raincoat styles: the earlier M1938 raincoat with ventilated back shield *(far right)*, a raincoat with corduroy collar *(third from right)*, and the simplified M1942 raincoat *(far left)* with straight back design.

The 1942-pattern experimental raincoat with double-coated fabric *(left)* worn beside sectional tent-poncho, a dual-purpose item that could be used either as a tent or a poncho *(right)*, during Quartermaster Board testing.

This prototype sectional tent poncho is being worn as a rain garment over the individual combat outfit, including full jungle pack, during early 1943 Quartermaster Board testing.

Experimental synthetic resin-coated raincoat of lengthened design worn with light individual combat equipment and gas-mask carrier during Quartermaster Board testing in early 1943.

# Enlisted Wool Overcoat

Machine gun crew of the 90th Inf Div, dressed in full-length 32-ounce melton wool overcoats, pauses along the route of march near Metzeresche, France, during November 1944. Wartime wool conservation measures mandated that overcoat material use a large proportion of reworked wool.

A veteran of the Huertgen Forest battle wears the olive-drab 32-ounce melton wool overcoat with overshoes. The wool overcoat was considered unsuitable for active campaigning, but it was issued to front-line troops during the 1944–45 winter campaign because cold-weather field garments were in short supply.

A soldier wears the overcoat as he moves along positions in the Montschau sector, facing the Westwall, during November 1944. This rear view shows the buttoned backstrap design.

Pvt. David Hibbit of the 83d Inf Div wears a typically snow-encrusted overcoat along with cartridge belt and attached M1 bayonet during the Ardennes counteroffensive. He is digging ice out of his canteen, near Lierneux, Belgium, in January 1945.

During January 1945 a soldier of the 26th Inf Div near the Wiltz River wears overcoat and blanket for warmth as he uses the soldier's standard eating receptacle, the meat can with its top part set aside. The handle, seen extended, was folded before the cup was placed in the canteen. The canteen-and-cup combination was carried in the canteen cover as a component of each soldier's individual equipment.

The double-breasted olive-drab melton wool overcoat *(left)* was normally reserved as part of the enlisted soldier's dress wardrobe. The army wanted to replace it with the M1943 long field overcoat *(right)*, but wartime materials and time were not available to supply desired quantities. As a result, it became restricted to commissioned officers, warrant officers, and contract surgeons.

The melton wool overcoat *(left)* was unsatisfactory for marching and too clumsy for combat conditions. The M1943 long field overcoat *(right)* was also deficient as a combat garment, but it filled a need for sentries, drivers, and personnel on furlough who needed rain protection as well as warmth. The ETO command found it particularly desirable for mechanics, who could not wear ponchos. Unfortunately, procurement difficulties prevented its distribution to enlisted ranks.

The standard melton wool overcoat used in full marching order *(left)*, compared to the M1943 experimental long field overcoat *(right)* used in the same role. The experimental garment was considered superior to the standard overcoat by the Quartermaster General, but deemed unnecessary for combat troops and unjustifiable as an enlisted-issue item because of textile shortages.

# Cold-Weather Clothing

The 1926-pattern short overcoat for commissioned officers *(left)* worn during February 1943 maneuvers. The sleeve ornamentation, two bands of black braid, signified a general officer. The center Marine officer has a winter combat jacket, and the army colonel *(right)* wears the M1941 field jacket.

Officers assembled at Fort McClellan, Alabama, in December 1943 wear *(left to right)* long field overcoat buttoned to the top, M1941 field jacket, special officer's short overcoat with belt but without notched lapels, private-purchase long field overcoat with additional yoke, and officer's short wool overcoat of 1926 pattern with added belt.

Generals conferring in Lunéville, France, during January 1945 have various coats and jackets *(left to right):* Lt. Gen. Jacob Devers in Air Force B-10 intermediate jacket; Lt. Gen. Brehon Somervell in private-purchase field overcoat with buckled straps; Lt. Gen. Alexander Patch in M1943 field jacket; and Lt. Gen. John C. H. Lee in standard wool field jacket.

Lt. Gen. George Patton Jr. *(left)* wears a personalized general officer's belt with his winter combat jacket, modified by adding shoulder straps, while meeting with Gen. Dwight Eisenhower *(right)*, who is dressed in a privately tailored field overcoat during the March 1943 Tunisian offensive.

During December 1943 Gen. Dwight Eisenhower wears his privately tailored long field overcoat with two-button sleeve straps as he views British 46th Div positions in Italy with Maj. Gen. J. L. T. Hawkesworth, seen wearing British 1940-pattern utility battle dress.

The M1943 officer's long field overcoat was designed like a trenchcoat, and could be worn in *capote* fashion with front coattails buttoned back to provide the knees with freedom of movement during marching. The overcoat had a buttoned-in, removable wool lining.

The M1943 officer's long field overcoat was practical in either garrison or field mode, as shown here. This otherwise nondescript officer carrying a standard M1 Garand rifle could still be detected by knowledgeable enemy snipers, because the coat was not issued to enlisted ranks.

Rear view of the M1943 officer's long field overcoat worn with combat field pack (the redesignated jungle pack) and experimental collapsible canteen, showing the single plait extending down the center of the back.

Captain Magarth wears the M1943 officer's long field overcoat at Le Havre, France, during February 1945.

On Iceland during November 1942, a 40mm antiaircraft gun is manned by 494th Coast Artillery Bn members attired in alpaca-lined, full-length overcoats styled like parkas with permanently attached hoods.

A corps commander *(right)*, dressed in decorated helmet liner with pile-lined parka-type overcoat, inspects battle damage sustained to the helmet of a soldier *(left)*, who is wearing a raincoat and leather-palm wool gloves.

During January 1945 in Cherbourg, France, Corp. Anthony Mancia *(right)* wears the 1938-version original mackinaw coat with wool collar and belt, while Sergeant Bell *(left)* has the revised plain mackinaw. Note M1903 .30 cal. Springfield rifle and overshoes.

Military police guarding the 30th Inf Div command post in Malmédy, Belgium, wear the winter combat jacket *(left)* and third-pattern mackinaw coat without belt loops. Conservation of cotton duck material forced the army to replace the original 10.2-ounce waterproofed duck, used as the outer fabric of the mackinaw, with a lighter cotton fabric that readily soaked up water.

Attired in typical winter clothing with shoe pacs, 6th Cavalry Group troops prepare to attack the West Wall in February 1945. Sgt. Eugene Jones *(left front)* wears cloth bandoleer across High Neck sweater and shirt with winter combat trousers. Corp. Vernon King *(center)* has M1 rifle ammunition clip on bandoleer strap over M1943 field jacket. Note his wool ski socks and shoe pacs. Corp. Joseph Gregor *(right)* wears winter combat jacket and trousers, ripped at knee and showing wool trousers underneath.

Senior general's attire is shown in this October 1944 picture of 6th Army Group Lt. Gen. Jacob Devers *(right)*, wearing Eighth Air Force ETO-style wool field jacket, meeting with Lt. Gen. Lucian Truscott *(center)*, in regular wool field jacket, and Lt. Gen. Alexander Patch, who has a commercial leather jacket.

1Lt. Julian Wright, a liaison pilot with the 1st Inf Div, used the air force heavy winter alpaca pile B-11 jacket while on reconnaissance missions over Honnef in the Rhineland during March 1945.

Pilot SSgt. Robert Lee wears an air force B-10 intermediate jacket beside his liaison aircraft in Belgium during January 1945.

Preparing for an artillery observation flight over the Saarland in January 1945, *(left to right)* SSgt. Lee Leggett wears alpaca-lined parka overcoat, Lt. George Lawler uses an air force B-6 shearling jacket, and SSgt. Frank Hassie has a type B-3 shearling jacket.

# *Mountain/Ski Clothing and Cold-Weather Items*

Army troops outfitted in snow coveralls fire a toboggan-mounted M1917 Browning .30 cal. heavy machine gun during 1941 training in the northern United States. Their headgear *(left to right):* the special-procurement civilian-type ski cap, the M1937 winter cap, and the M1907 winter cap.

Army ski and snowshoe patrol garbed in white ski trousers and parkas firing from the prone position.

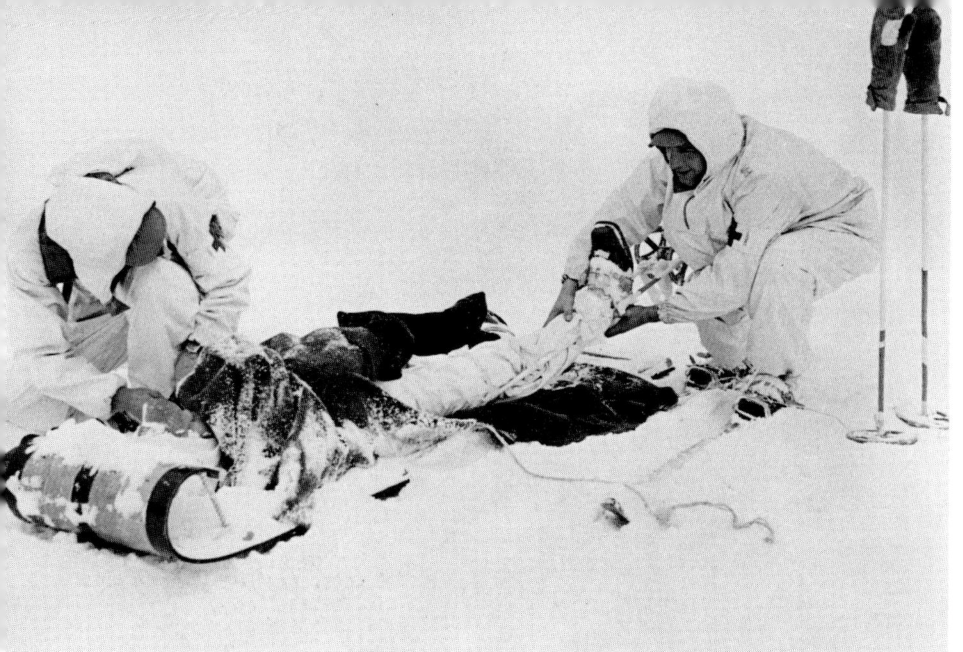

Army ski troops secure an injured comrade to a toboggan for evacuation while training in the United States. Note mitten shells on ski poles.

During 1943 winter maneuvers an army ski trooper emerges from a dugout flanked by trail snowshoes and hickory steel-edged skis, complete with Kandahar-type ski bindings.

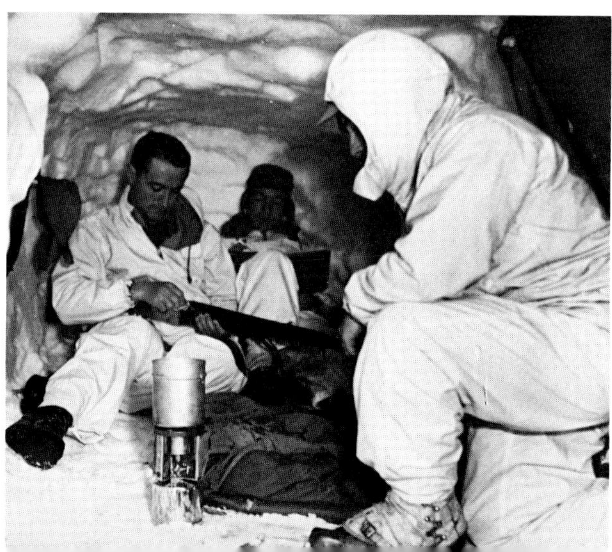

Ski troops wearing M1941 reversible ski parkas and white ski trousers use the M1941 mountain stove. The soldier in foreground wears the ski gaiter, a short canvas legging used to prevent snow from entering the top of mountain boot.

Armor troops dressed in field cotton parkas worn over pile parkas, along with prototype goggles and trigger-finger mitten shells, test clothing inside an M5 light tank while serving with the Armored Board Winter Detachment at Camp McCoy, Wisconsin.

Arctic zone–equipped troops of the 808th Tank Destroyer Bn wearing pile field jacket *(left)* and fur-trimmed reversible ski parkas use canvas tubes of a Herman-Nelson heater to dry their mountain sleeping bags and cases and their shoe pacs.

Prototype goggles. Inhaled air was drawn through replaceable filter felts *(right)*, which prevented direct air blasts against the eye and filtered out debris. The air swept the lens chamber and surface, removing moisture before fogging the lens, and then passed through the inlet valve and into the nose. Exhaling closed the inlet valve and opened the outlet valve at the base of the nosepiece, while the rubber shield and one-way inlet valve blocked the return of moisture-laden exhaled breath into the lens chamber.

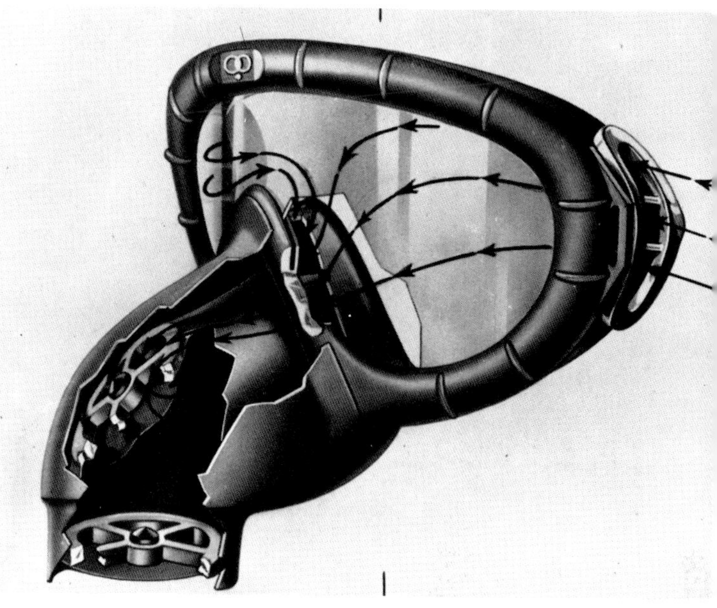

The unsatisfactory chamois cold-weather face mask worn with ski goggles by a soldier dressed in the M1943 field jacket and trigger-finger mitten shells. The soft chamois leather mask had an adjustable elastic strap that fitted under the chin. The mask came with mouth slit and nose flap, but the soldier had to cut out eye holes to conform with his features.

Prototype ski and mountain goggles had green-tinted glass lenses that filtered out ultraviolet, infrared, and excessive light rays. The goggles effectively eliminated glare and relieved eyestrain in a snow environment, and were modified slightly by adding white-colored side shielding cloth before standardization.

The test-pattern field pile parka had a pile lining and wolverine trim on the hood. Designed for wear under the cotton field parka, the pile parka was modified before standardization so that both could be put on and taken off without removing one from the other.

The prototype field cotton parka was a long-skirted, hooded jacket that formed the windproof outer shell for severe cold conditions. The field parka, here worn over the field pile parka, was standardized after shortening to raise the lower closure to waist level. The longer version was modified by adding fur trimming to the hood and became the reversible ski parka.

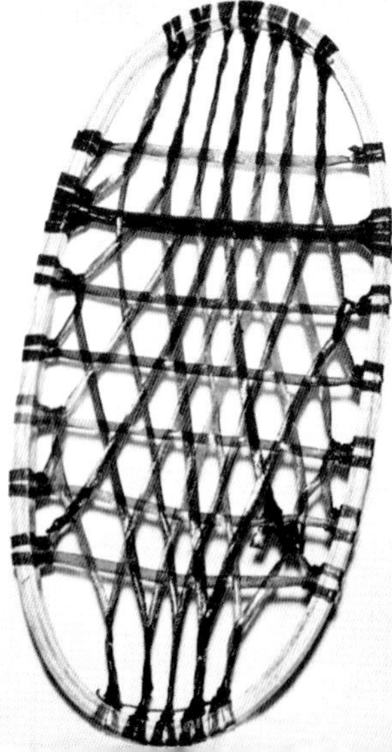

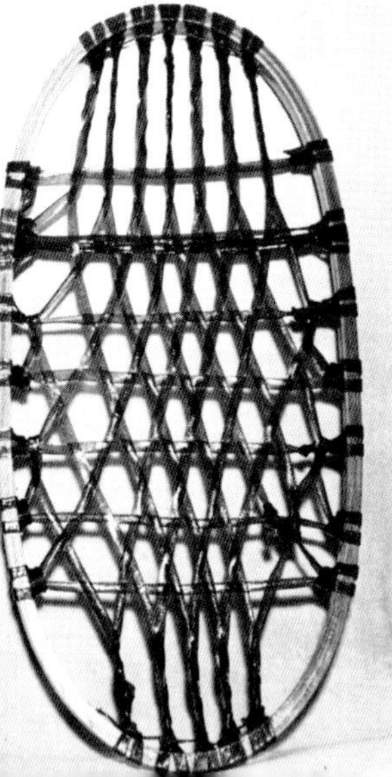

The small emergency snowshoes were adopted to give troops traction in deep snow where skis were impractical or not available, such as during combat or in cross-country treks after a vehicle became stalled. The foot was strapped flat on the snowshoe, and walking became tiresome if used for long distances.

Clothing experts believed that one multi-functional battle combination, using flexible layers, could replace most specialized arctic and cold-climate garments. The pile field jacket had outside rayon facing and was lined with a 50-50 mohair and alpaca blend, and was adopted as a liner for the M1943 field jacket.

*(Above)* The lower portion of the wool serge field trousers, showing the button tabs. The trousers were designed for ordinary cold weather, and could also be worn under the cotton trousers to give added warmth in very cold weather.

Field cotton sateen trousers were designed as wind-resistant and water-repellent outer shells for use over the wool field trousers in cold-weather regions. These trousers being demonstrated at Pine Camp, New York, show the lower straps securing the ankle closure.

An infantryman of the 65th Inf Div wears the olive-drab wool muffler, a soft lightly brushed piece of wool four feet long and one foot wide, during March 1945.

Capt. William Griffin composes a letter near Nancy, France, during October 1944. He is wearing the officer's winter service shirt with scarf worn in ascot fashion.

A 34th Inf Div lieutenant wears the division insignia on his scarf-ascot during the Italian campaign of December 1944. The static nature of the Italian front produced more individualized unit items of this nature than the fluid situation in northern Europe.

The first officer to cross Remagen Bridge over the Rhine, Lt. Karl Timmermann of the 9th Arm Div, wears a pullover sweater from Red Cross relief clothing sources under his combat uniform. For a variety of reasons, local procurement of additional cold-weather clothing for U.S. units in continental Europe, especially within the French region, was almost nonexistent.

The trigger-finger mitten insert was designed to be worn inside the mitten shell. The prototype version in this picture was tested by the Armored Board Winter Detachment at Pine Camp, New York

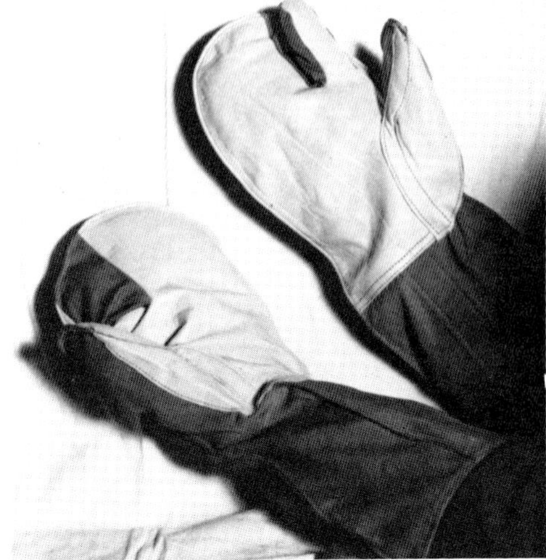

Trigger-finger mitten shells were leather-palm mitts with a windproof poplin backing and gauntlets that were used along with the mitten inserts. The flexible finger design permitted a soldier to fire his weapon without exposing his hand to frigid conditions. However, drivers complained that the shell slipped off the insert and often prevented them from grasping the wheel properly.

Sgt. Joseph Holmes of the 35th Inf Div wears the winter combat helmet, a cotton windproof head covering with wool jersey lining, under his M1 helmet assembly at the Belgian front during January 1945. Note leather-palm wool gloves.

# 5

# Armor and Airborne Attire

The army initiated development of specialized clothing for armored-vehicle crewmen in 1940 and concentrated on jackets and trousers that would provide warmth but not interfere with obstructions within the tanks, both for safety of movement and ease of emergency exiting. For these reasons, cold-weather tanker uniforms had to be less cumbersome than the layered winter combat ensembles being developed for other troops. An assembly for tankers was developed in the following year and extensively field tested by the Armored Winter Board Detachment at Camp Pine, New York.

Based on the carefully monitored experience of testing personnel at Camp Pine, final garments were selected and tentative Quartermaster Corps specifications were approved in March and June 1942 for a winter combat jacket, wool-lined combat trousers, and a winter combat helmet. The short, windproof, water-repellent winter combat jacket was made of 20-ounce olive-drab suiting lined with wool. It was stylish in appearance and fitted snugly because of its knitted wool waistband, cuff, and neck openings. The winter combat trousers had a high bib front and suspenders, and were made of cotton lined with wool jersey. The chin-fastened helmet was designed mainly to protect crewmen from hazardous objects in the tank's interior.

The Armored Force clothing was considered highly efficient and attractive, and most army personnel engaged in winter fighting tried to secure the jacket for their own use. The army, however, disapproved its wider distribution on the basis that the jackets were specifically designed for working in the closed turrets and hulls of tanks, and had sacrificed the necessary layers of warmth needed for general cold-climate work.

The army organized its first parachute unit in 1940 as an air-delivered extension of the infantry, and recognized the immediate need for highly specialized clothing and gear for the airborne troops. The first quartermaster clothing developed for the paratroopers consisted of a one-piece green garment made of wind-resistant "balloon-cloth," or green "silk" sateen. The original suit presented numerous combat-efficiency problems ranging from the bright sheen and snagging nature of its material to the poorly designed pockets and tendency of zippers to malfunction.

During 1941 a two-piece jumpsuit was offered as an alternative uniform by a board of officers from the Fort Benning-based Provisional Parachute Group that included Maj. Theodore Dunn, Maj. Robert Sink, Maj. George Millett, Capt. William Yarborough, Capt. Charles Billingslea, and Capt. James Bassett. These officers jointly developed a new cotton poplin parachute jumper's coat patterned after the field jacket but modified by enlarged "slash" breast pockets, and high-waist parachute jumper's trousers of similar material, with additional cargo and side pockets. The trousers were also tapered to stay inside the boots. The uniform was adopted in 1942 and, with the exception of certain measures undertaken in March 1943 to strengthen the trouser leg pockets, remained standard paratrooper issue for the duration of the war.

Paratroopers were outfitted initially with soft aviation helmets, but parachuting exposed the jumpers to increased risk of head injury. The search for a rigid, head-protective shell led to the early investigation of "Riddell helmets"—plastic football helmets invented by equipment designer John T. Riddell—that eventually proved unsatisfactory for combatant purposes. The paratroopers finally adopted the standard M1 helmet assembly after a special liner and fittings were installed to prevent it from coming off during the parachute descent. A special suspension system, including chin strap and protective leather chin cup, enabled the helmet to absorb the sudden jolt of the opening parachute, remain free from tangled shroud lines, and stay secured to the paratrooper's head.

Another urgent task was developing footwear that could properly sustain the paratrooper's impact with the ground, and ankle-braced boots with extra-high leather uppers and rubber soles were initially recommended. Eventually a simpler boot was designed; it retained high-laced leather support but deleted the ankle supports and much of the rubber cushioning. Tentative specifications for the new parachute jumper's boot were adopted in April 1942, and it rapidly became another cherished hallmark of the special paratrooper uniform.

# Armored Troops

Motorcyclist summer garrison dress uniform of 1941 included cotton khaki shirt and service breeches, aviator's summer flying helmet with goggles, riding gloves, and high-laced leather boots first issued to mounted troops in 1931. Specialist apparel was issued personnel such as motorcyclists, armored crewmen, parachutists, and medical troops.

Observation post of the 13th Inf in October 1941 includes a forward scout in motorcycle helmet with goggles *(front)*. Signalman in helmet *(center)* is equipped with training gas mask slung over his back and resting beside canteen.

Maj. Gen. George Patton Jr. observes M2 light tanks while wearing the rigid football-type tanker helmet and the original-style combat winter jacket, an attractively designed, short, snug jacket made of 20-ounce olive-drab suiting lined with wool.

A tank commander in the 5th Arm Div wears the tanker's M1942 winter combat helmet with ventilated crown while in the turret of a Sherman M4 medium tank, beside a .30 cal. antiaircraft machine gun, during fall 1943 maneuvers at Pine Camp, New York.

SSgt. Roy Grubbe of the 4th Arm Div near Chambéry, France, during October 1944, wears the standard tanker's winter combat helmet along with goggles. The helmet was designed to protect crew members against sharp objects and metal protrusions inside the confines of a tank, and was constructed of hard fiber padded with leather. He also wears the winter combat jacket.

Tank crewman, dressed in standard winter wool shirt and trousers along with the tanker's winter combat helmet, surveys rising water near his tarped-over M4 Sherman medium tank during a November 1944 rainstorm in France.

Cavalry reconnaissance personnel of the 1st Arm Div wear M1943 field jackets and standard tanker's helmets as they cross the Po River on an M5 light tank in Italy during April 1945.

A medical aidman wears the winter combat trousers portion of the Armored Force winter combat suit (without the jacket) while tending a wounded infantryman. The cotton trousers were designed like overalls with a high front bib. The overshoes were unpopular because rubber shortages had forced the army to use standard cloth material that tore and leaked easily. Many units discarded the overshoes altogether because the clumsy footwear retarded fast movement.

*(Below)* The assistant commander of the 70th Inf Div, Brig. Gen. Thomas Herren, wears the winter combat jacket with modified shoulder straps, showing the wool lining, in March 1945. The jacket closed with a single zipper and had two slit pockets. Note pistol belt with magazine pocket and compass case.

*(Above)* Medical aidman of the 102d Cav Group with Distinguished Service Cross near Rott, Germany, in December 1944. He wears the M1936 ammunition belt suspenders with pistol belt, as well as the medical kit bag with carrying strap, over his winter combat jacket.

*(Right)* Col. John Higgins, being decorated in Germany during March 1945, is dressed in the second-model winter combat jacket authorized in March 1942. The jacket had knitted wool wristlets, collar, and waistband. It could be easily worn over most clothing as weather demanded, including combinations of woolen underwear, wool trousers and shirt, and herringbone twill outfits. Note private-purchase shoulder holster.

# Parachutist Clothing

The experimental green "silk" parachute jumper's suit, known informally as balloon-cloth jump overalls, with Riddell crash helmet. The shiny sateen garment contained various pockets for grenades, pistol magazines, and other equipment.

Green "silk" parachute jumper's suit, showing talon fasteners. Extensive field tests revealed that the suit was impractical as a standard parachuting outfit.

*(Left)* Paratrooper duty dress of late 1940 consisted of first-model mechanic's coveralls, early paratrooper boots with ankle straps, and garrison cap with infantry blue piping and parachute disc. These were the first dress distinctions before authorization of jump wings. At this stage of uniform development, the oversea cap was the mark of armor or parachutist personnel, while regular infantry wore service hats.

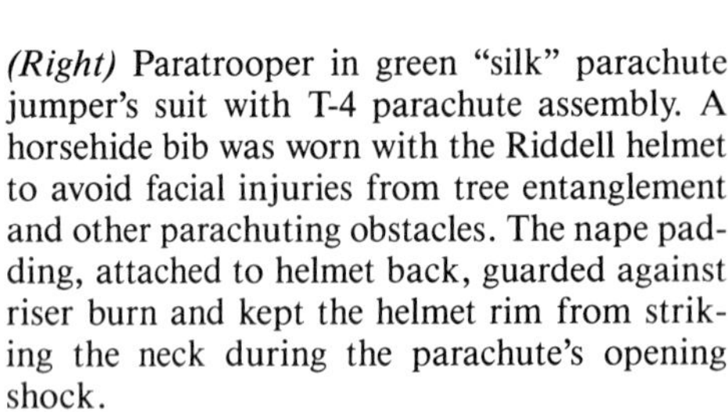

*(Right)* Paratrooper in green "silk" parachute jumper's suit with T-4 parachute assembly. A horsehide bib was worn with the Riddell helmet to avoid facial injuries from tree entanglement and other parachuting obstacles. The nape padding, attached to helmet back, guarded against riser burn and kept the helmet rim from striking the neck during the parachute's opening shock.

Members of the 501st Parachute Bn chute up at Lawson Field in August 1941, wearing the green "silk" parachute suits. The front paratrooper putting on parachute harness has the type A-8 intermediate helmet, a cloth toque that preceded other headgear, while his assistant wears the Riddell helmet.

Comparison of the green "silk" parachutist uniform *(right)* with summer motorcyclist uniform *(center)* and the Armored Force outfit with winter combat jacket and helmet *(left)*.

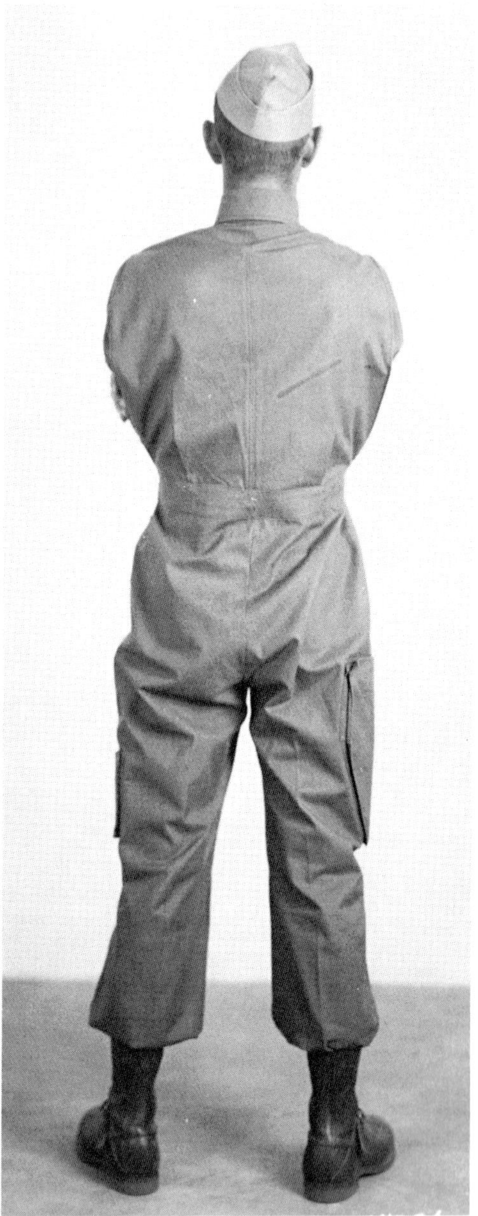

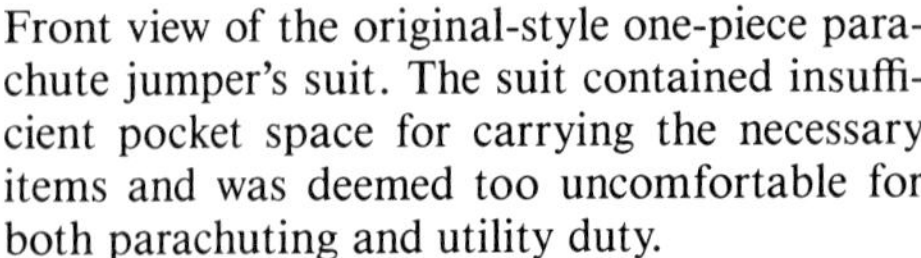
Front view of the original-style one-piece parachute jumper's suit. The suit contained insufficient pocket space for carrying the necessary items and was deemed too uncomfortable for both parachuting and utility duty.

Back view of the original-model, one-piece parachute jumper's suit. This view shows the lack of fullness in the seat and the snug waist fitting that inhibited parachuting flexibility.

Parachute jumper's suit, modification no. 1. The two-piece suit with slash pockets was preferred, although a standing collar was retained to give protection around the neck region. This was the model that provided the basis for the standardized parachute jumper's coat and trousers.

Parachute jumper's suit, modification no. 2. In this alternative, the placement of the slash pockets on the breast was not favored because it failed to facilitate the natural entrance of the hands. However, the location of the patch pockets on the thigh was considered superior to the first modification.

Parachute jumper's suit, modification no. 3. The snugness, fixed belt, and breeches were all disapproved, although the ample roominess of the lower coat pockets became the standard for pocket design enlargements.

Paratrooper chaplain Raymond Hall at Fort Benning, Georgia, wears the M1942 parachute jumper's coat over winter service shirt, with U.S. and branch insignia worn on collar, during April 1942. This photograph shows the transition of uniform items: the earlier Riddell helmet and nape protective padding are still being used alongside the coat's final slanted large-pocket design.

During 1943 these paratroopers under arms at Camp Mackall, North Carolina, wear the winter service shirt and trousers with garrison cap *(left)* and the M1942 parachute jumper suit with M1 helmet assembly *(right)*. Note metal jump wings worn by both individuals.

Paratrooper of the 509th Parachute Inf regiment in Italy during 1944, wearing the M1942 parachutist suit modified by elbow and knee patches with openings for insertion of brown-felt padding, as well as field-expedient spray paint camouflaging. His equipment includes M1936 canvas field bag, first aid packet on suspenders, and pistol belt with attached pocket magazine, M1910 canteen, and M1943 intrenching shovel.

Back view of a paratrooper from the 509th Parachute Inf regiment in Italy, showing the M1936 canvas field bag that was developed initially for mechanized troops and widely known as the musette bag. A five-magazine Thompson ammunition pocket carrier, used for 20-round magazines, is worn underneath. He also has an M1943 intrenching shovel and an M3 trench knife tucked behind holster.

Lt. Gen. Mark Clark decorates paratrooper captain in Italy. The captain is wearing the M1942 parachutist suit in combat garrison mode, with pistol belt, M1936 ammunition belt suspenders, and compass case.

Paratroopers of the 502d Parachute Inf with Gen. Dwight Eisenhower before the D-Day invasion of June 1944, wearing the M1942 parachutist suits and camouflage-netted helmets. Paratrooper on right is wearing general-purpose ammunition bag over chest, and paratrooper wearing the "23" aircraft manifest tag has a Hawkins light antitank mine strapped to lower leg.

Paratrooper wearing T-5 parachute assembly, with Thompson submachine gun slung underneath belly band, climbs aboard aircraft for the D-Day airborne assault. He has several Thompson magazine bags taped together with electrical tape as well as a canvas field bag below reserve parachute. Note M3 trench knife strapped to lower leg, and the chin strap for the helmet liner pulled over helmet.

Glider troops of the 1st Airborne Task Force (Provisional 7th Army A/B Div) board aircraft for the air assault into southern France during August 1944. They wear parachutist uniforms, some of them splotch-painted, as well as life vests. Note center soldier wearing sweater.

During September 1944, 82d A/B Div personnel prepare for the parachute assault into Holland. The paratrooper *(second from left)* has M1943 field jacket and first aid pouch tied onto cartridge belt, with pack suspenders tied to restrain loose ends. Paratrooper *(right)* has transition-type intrenching shovel cover, with dark green edging on khaki body.

Members of the 17th A/B Div, equipped with T-5 parachutes, board a C-46 aircraft for the air drop east of the Rhine River near Wesel in March 1945.

# 6

# Women's Clothing

The establishment of the Women's Army Auxiliary Corps (WAAC) in early 1942, expanded and redesignated as the Women's Army Corps (WAC) during September 1943, was an unexpected development that caught the Quartermaster Corps unprepared to produce suitable wartime clothing for women quickly. The first designs were rushed into production by officers unfamiliar with the women's clothing field. They received plenty of advice and consultation, but ultimately failed to hire the experts required to create a satisfactory line of dress, field, and working attire. The whole endeavor was given such low priority that a women's clothing section did not even exist in the quartermaster's research and development branch until the last year of the war.

The basic women's uniforms consisted of six-gore skirts and single-breasted jackets with four pockets and a self-belt, primarily fabricated from materials, such as heavy canvas and haircloth, that proved completely unsuitable for proper fitting. In July 1942, the new garments were issued to the first WAAC personnel at Fort Des Moines, Iowa, and immediately prompted severe criticism. The clothing was so defective that a satisfactory women's uniform was achieved only after years of extensive pattern revisions.

When the WAAC was first created, its personnel were authorized to wear appropriate civilian dress for unofficial social or formal evening functions. The practice was disallowed after September 1943, when the WAC branch was formalized and wearing military jacket and skirt became mandatory on all occasions. Suggestions for an off-duty dress were not followed until the spring of 1944, when the Quartermaster Corps formally seconded the recommendation. After the usual difficulties in choosing fabric, color, and design, a wool crepe off-duty dress in military beige coloration was standardized. Although the final product suffered from some faulty fabric and dye choices, the overall result was capable of modification and met the requirement adequately.

An enlarged Army Nurse Corps (ANC), by contrast, was anticipated before hostilities began, but work in this field was slow at first and not coordinated with ongoing programs to outfit other female soldiers. By the fall of 1942 this situation was being corrected, and eventually the same service uniforms, coats, shirtwaists, neckties, stockings, and gloves were stocked for both WAC and ANC. At that stage of the war the only distinctive nursing uniform components consisted of the caps, nurse's handbag, and the ANC insignia itself. The tidy white hospital uniforms, traditionally associated with the role of nurse since World War I, were replaced by more functional brown-and-white woven seersucker dresses that wrapped around with a tie belt. The nurse seersucker uniforms, to which a jacket and cap were eventually added, were employed first overseas, then extended to stateside facilities in mid-1944.

Women's field clothing became especially critical as the war progressed and women specialists, as well as nurses, were placed in forward locations under battle conditions. In the North African and early Italian campaigns, combat work garments specifically designed for women were still unavailable, and female soldiers were forced to wear men's jackets, herringbone twill suits, and boots. The unsatisfactory sizing differences often caused discomfort, difficulties in duty performance, and less than ideal protection against wind or adverse weather.

In response, field suits for women were manufactured in a one-piece herringbone twill fatigue style and a trousers and jacket set. The exercise suit, a simple front-button dress with tie sash, was even pressed into service as makeshift utility attire. While these suits proved sufficient for summer wear, cold-weather items became imperative as more and more women became active in winter duties either outdoors or in unheated vehicles and structures. The Quartermaster Corps adopted the layering principle already proven in male clothing to produce a line of winter apparel that included women's field jackets, hoods, outer cover trousers, wool liners, gloves, and underwear. One of the main differences in women's arctic clothing, however, was that their battle jackets had wool liners rather than the pile liners used in men's jackets.

Like their male counterparts, women had to await adequate tropical clothing development. Tropical wear was delayed in the quartermaster rush to compose cold-weather and arctic ensembles. Thus, women soldiers suffered through most Pacific campaigns garbed in either seersucker slacks-and-shirt combinations or cotton herringbone twill fatigues, both of which offered scant protection from mosquitoes. Repeated requests for khaki shirts and slacks were not met until very late in the war.

# *Formal Attire*

Original uniforms of the Women's Army Auxiliary Corps, as authorized in July 1942 *(left to right):* dark olive-drab officer's jacket with khaki skirt, officer's khaki summer uniform, and winter auxiliary uniform. The first coats included belts despite a March decision not to include them, but revised patterns adopted in October eliminated the belts.

Second-pattern WAAC jacket was a beltless, fitted garment that contained dummy pockets with flaps instead of the original patch pockets. It is being modeled with darker-colored navy WAVE uniforms on New York's Fifth Avenue in early 1943. The navy avoided the army's issue-clothing problems by granting WAVEs a uniform allowance that enabled them to secure clothing of department-store quality.

WAAC director Oveta Hobby and Commandant Don Faith inspect the first officer candidate class at Fort Des Moines, Iowa, in August 1942. The officer candidates are dressed in hot stiff cotton jackets and WAAC "hobby hats." Note how the heavy cotton khaki skirts buckled and wrinkled across the stomach, so that even the slimmest WAAC presented a bloated appearance after she had sat down once.

The WAC band at Daytona Beach training center, wearing dark barathea skirts and winter caps, march past a formation in full summer dress. The unfashionable appearance of the original WAC uniforms is evident.

Women auxiliaries dressed in first-pattern skirts and cotton shirtwaists with neckties, while wearing headphones in simulation of combat tracking tasks. The early skirts were cut on a straight line instead of rounded at the hips, making them uncomfortably tight with a tendency to creep up in front, as shown at left.

Members of the Women's Army Corps gather on the parade field with Joseph Grew at Fort Oglethorpe, Georgia, during November 1943. They wear the third-pattern WAC wool winter jackets *(left)* and officer's wool jackets with shoulder loops *(right)*. Both types had dummy upper pockets with buttoned flaps and two slit pockets on the lower front.

Capt. Helen Hart, Chemical Warfare Service, wearing the early-pattern summer uniform jacket with shoulder straps and WAAC eagle on officer's summer cap during August 1943.

Capt. Alcesta Fowler with second-pattern uniform jacket with shoulder loops during September 1943.

Lt. Sally Goldstein, Transportation Corps, wears the garrison cap with the dark wool serge women's ETO jacket. Starting in October 1944, the coat and matching skirt or trousers were procured in England by theater command to supplement the WAC service uniform. The garments were extremely popular but limited to European issue during the war.

Lt. Mary Ann Gratto with wool barathea WAC officer's winter cap. Note WAC "Pallas Athene" lapel insignia.

Pvt. Alyca Nickles wears the WAC beige summer dress, an attractive off-duty dress made of summer-weight wool-crepe fabric with matched brown accessories of pumps, WAC utility bag, and gloves. The dress is worn with winter garrison cap.

Capt. Eleanor Fox wears the cotton poplin khaki shirtwaist.

During summer 1945 WAC Technician Dody Wilson and SSgt. Robert French relax in occupied Germany. She is wearing the WAC summer beige off-duty dress; he is wearing his uniform in highly informal fashion with shirt open, no necktie, and wool field jacket unbuttoned, giving a good view of the jacket's waist tab.

The summer tropical worsted duty uniform was not permitted for enlisted WACs until mid-1944, and initially was regarded as optional off-duty attire. Later it became an item of issue with maintenance at government expense, giving the WAC soldier a second summer dress uniform.

The simply designed, coat-style WAC hospital dress, made of a lightweight, durable cotton lawn fabric in tan shade, was standardized in January 1945.

# Field Attire

Women's one-piece herringbone twill suit *(left)* and special herringbone twill shirt and trousers *(right)* worn at Fort Oglethorpe, Georgia, during testing in the fall of 1943.

The bulkiness of the women's herringbone twill shirt and the looseness of its underarm portion are demonstrated during a WAC formation at Fort Oglethorpe, Georgia, in 1943. The WAC summer hats were made from khaki twill fabric.

Rear view of the women's herringbone twill shirt and trousers, showing the large proportions and excessive fullness that created discomfort and detracted from the appearance of both garments.

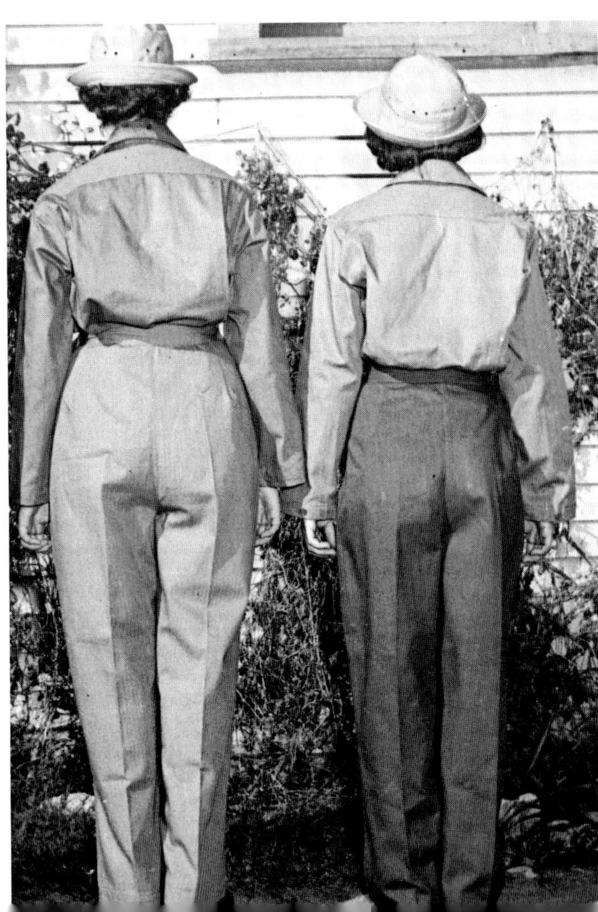

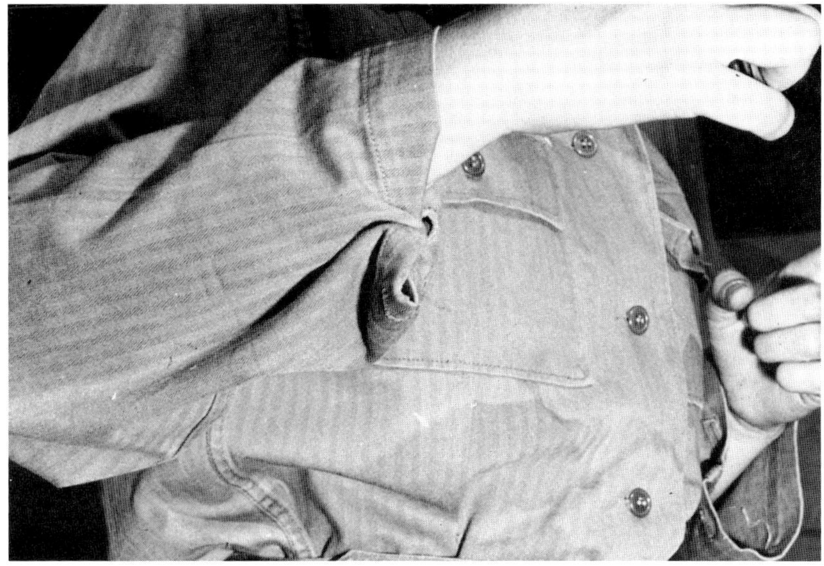

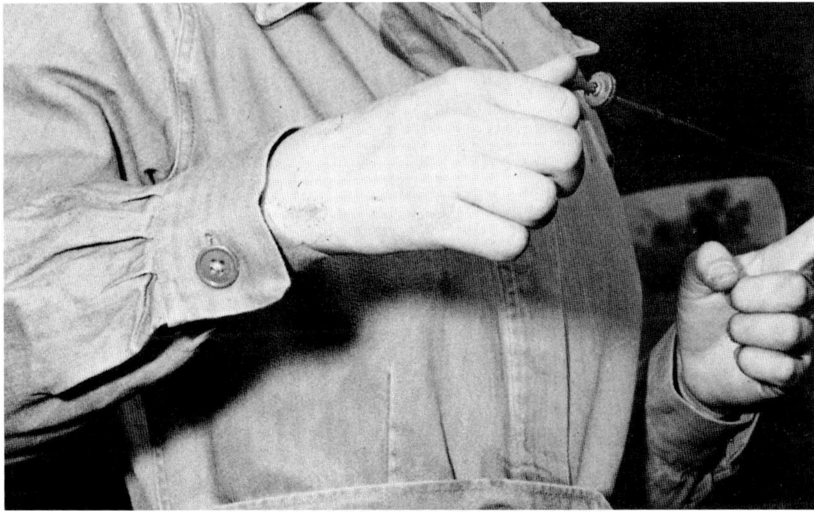

The wrist closure of the women's herringbone twill shirt *(top)* was unsatisfactory, even with its single buttonhole secured. In contrast, the one-piece herringbone twill work suit wrist closure *(bottom)* had a neater button fastening.

Laundering the women's herringbone twill two-piece work suit shrunk the sleeve and leg fabric, which made it difficult to assume a comfortable position while working. Note WAC summer hat.

Bending movement also strained the back material on the women's one-piece work suit *(right)*, often tearing buttons off the drop seat. The trousers of the two-piece suit *(left)* were unaffected by the same exercise.

Bending movement strained buttons and caused gaping in the hip closure of the women's one-piece herringbone twill work suit *(right);* the closure of the women's herringbone twill trousers stayed secure.

Combat nurse wearing women's outer cover trousers while sitting down, showing knee area restriction caused by wearing the stirrups over the feet as mandated. The women's arctic four-buckle overshoes could not be buckled completely when trousers were worn inside them.

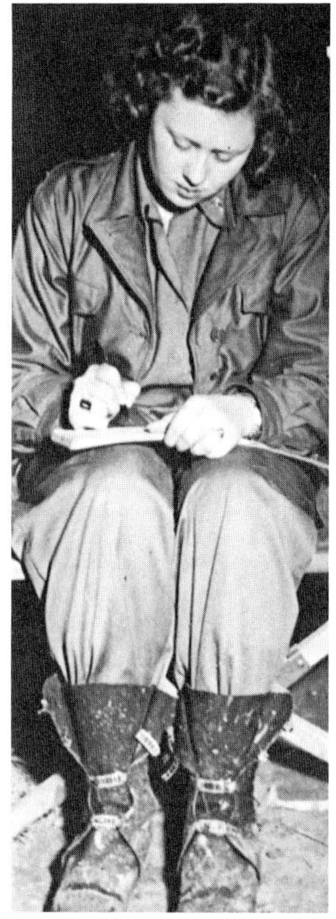

The women's outer cover trousers were wind-resistant and water-repellent slacks made of cotton fabric; they were designed to be worn over the women's wool liner trousers in cold climates. The trousers had adjustable waistband closures and elastic stirrups for fitting underneath footwear.

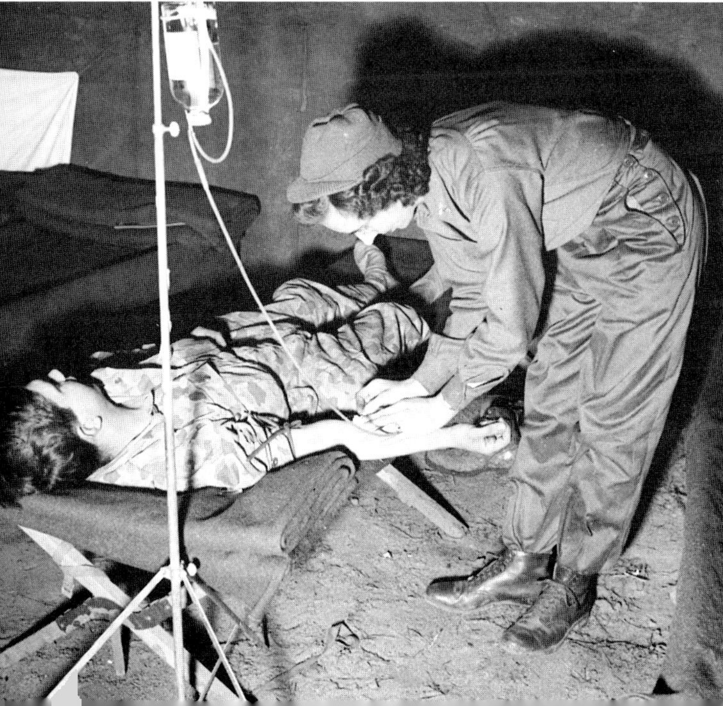

Army nurse wears the women's outer cover trousers over wool liner trousers, along with the women's wool waist with appropriate collar insignia and the wool knit cap. Note that side pocket opens when nurse bends over; when women sat down, articles often fell out of the pocket.

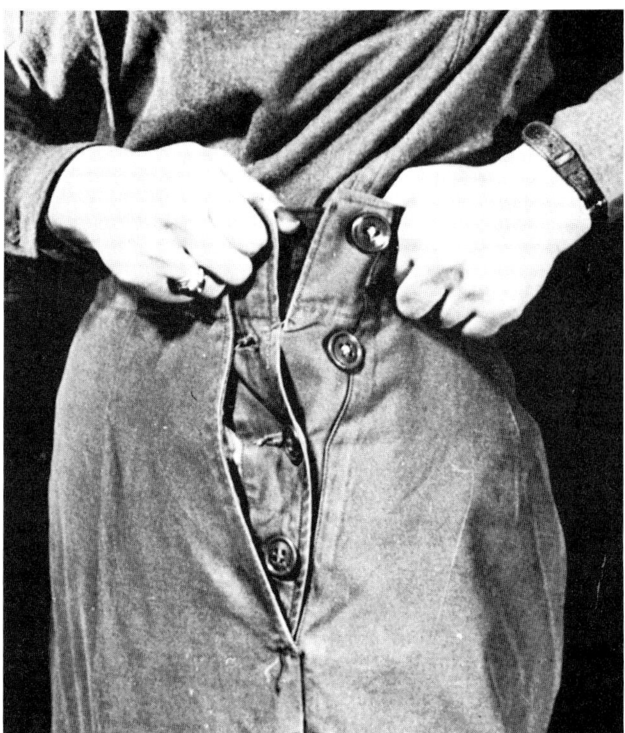

Women's outer cover trousers experienced frequent elastic stirrup failures and deterioration of the lower leg bottoms. Shrinkage often rendered the garments impractical for outer wear. After only three washings, the adjustable closure on the waistband shrunk so much that the top button could not be fastened.

The women's wool liner trousers had a knitted rib cuff at the ankle, and were worn under the women's outer cover trousers for extra warmth.

The women's wool liner trousers were fitted slacks that served either as a uniform outer component or as an extra garment for warmth under the outer cover trousers. The length of the wool liner, however, was inadequate to fit regular and long-size leg inseams. This nurse is 5 feet 6 inches tall with a 28-inch leg inseam, and is wearing size 14 wool liner trousers.

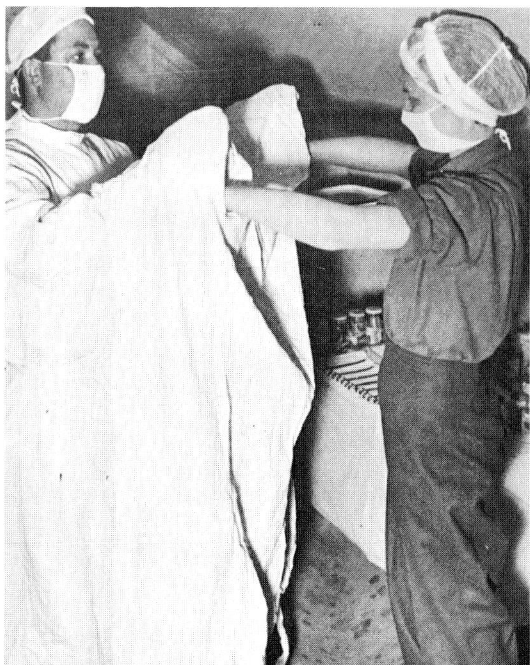

Nurse, wearing women's wool shirtwaist with sleeves rolled completely up, wool liner trousers, and a surgical head net, assists a doctor during a combat zone medical operation.

Women's tropical uniform consisted of cotton khaki slacks and matching shirt with convertible collar, worn with ankle-high shoes, khaki socks, and khaki oversea cap. The uniform was adopted late in the war to replace the herringbone twill fatigue clothing worn by women in the Southwest Pacific.

The women's wool shirtwaist was made of wool shirting flannel in the same style as the women's cotton shirtwaist, but was considered an ill-fitting garment with its oversized collars, shoulders, and sleeves.

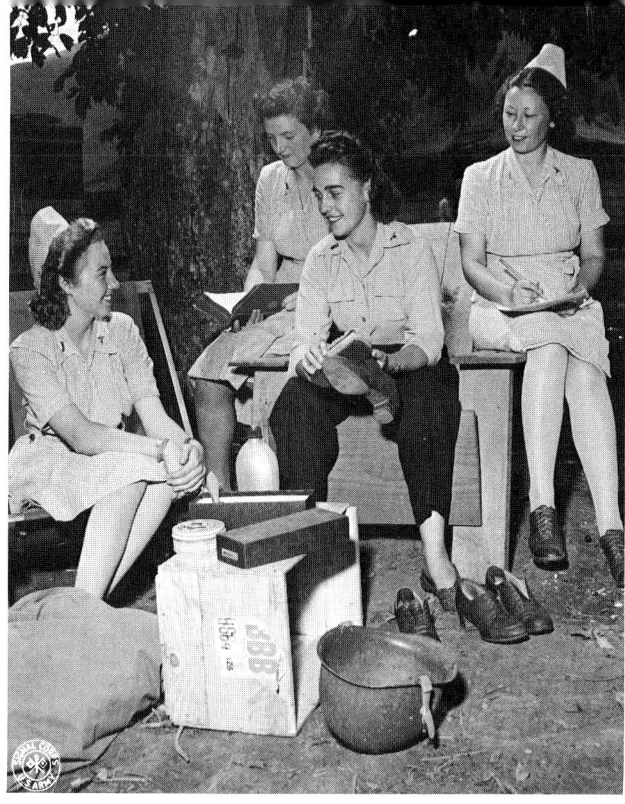


During February 1944 these nurses of the 29th General Hospital, stationed in the South Pacific, are dressed in women's cotton shirtwaists with women's dark summer slacks *(center)* and nurse's cotton seersucker uniforms. Note women's low service shoes.

Lt. Mary Allen wears the women's cotton shirtwaist with dark summer slacks *(left)*, while another officer *(right)* wears the nurse's cotton seersucker uniform, a wraparound hospital garment that closed at the waistline with a tie. Note nurse's seersucker cap.

The 8-ounce women's sweater *(top)* and 10-ounce women's sweater *(bottom)*. Both were popular rib-knit wool, hip-length sweaters with two lower front pockets. They were worn either over the basic uniform or as outer garments, and retained their fit after numerous washings.

A WAC weapons examiner test firing the .45 cal. M3 submachine gun, wearing the WAC exercise suit—a one-piece front-buttoned seersucker sport dress with short sleeves and self-belt. She is also wearing the khaki twill WAC summer "fatigue" or "Daisy Mae" hat.

# Cold-Weather Items

Women's M1943 field jacket was similar to the version issued to male soldiers except that the upper cargo pockets were deleted and a regular button front was substituted for the fly on the front closure.

The women's M1943 field jacket worn by a nurse with typical auxiliary equipment: pistol belt, canteen, and gas-mask carrier.

Women's M1943 field jacket detail, showing the difficulty of fastening the under-collar because the tab buttoning pushed the collar out of position and stretched the tab closure.

During July 1944 female personnel assembled at a field hospital in the Cotentin Peninsula of France wear the women's M1943 field jacket *(left)* and the Parsons M1941 field jacket *(center, holding helmet)*.

The women's field jacket hood was designed for a tight closure for cold-weather protection, but wearing earphones over the hood interfered with sound reception. Thus, headphones had to be worn like this female soldier in Alaska is doing, even though it caused the hood to bulge open. A loosely hanging hood created hazards inside confined vehicles, where it tended to catch on interior obstructions. This hood was small enough so that it could be folded easily and carried in the jacket's pocket when not in use.

The M1943 women's field jacket hood could be worn over the M1941 wool knit cap *(left)* or under the M1 helmet assembly *(right)*. In the latter position, the wool knit cap had been worn in a reversed position under the hood or else the cap's visor would cause gaping in the hood's facial fit.

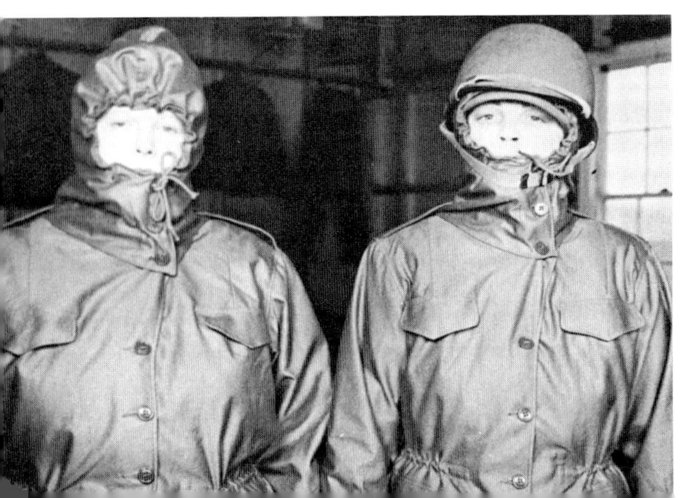

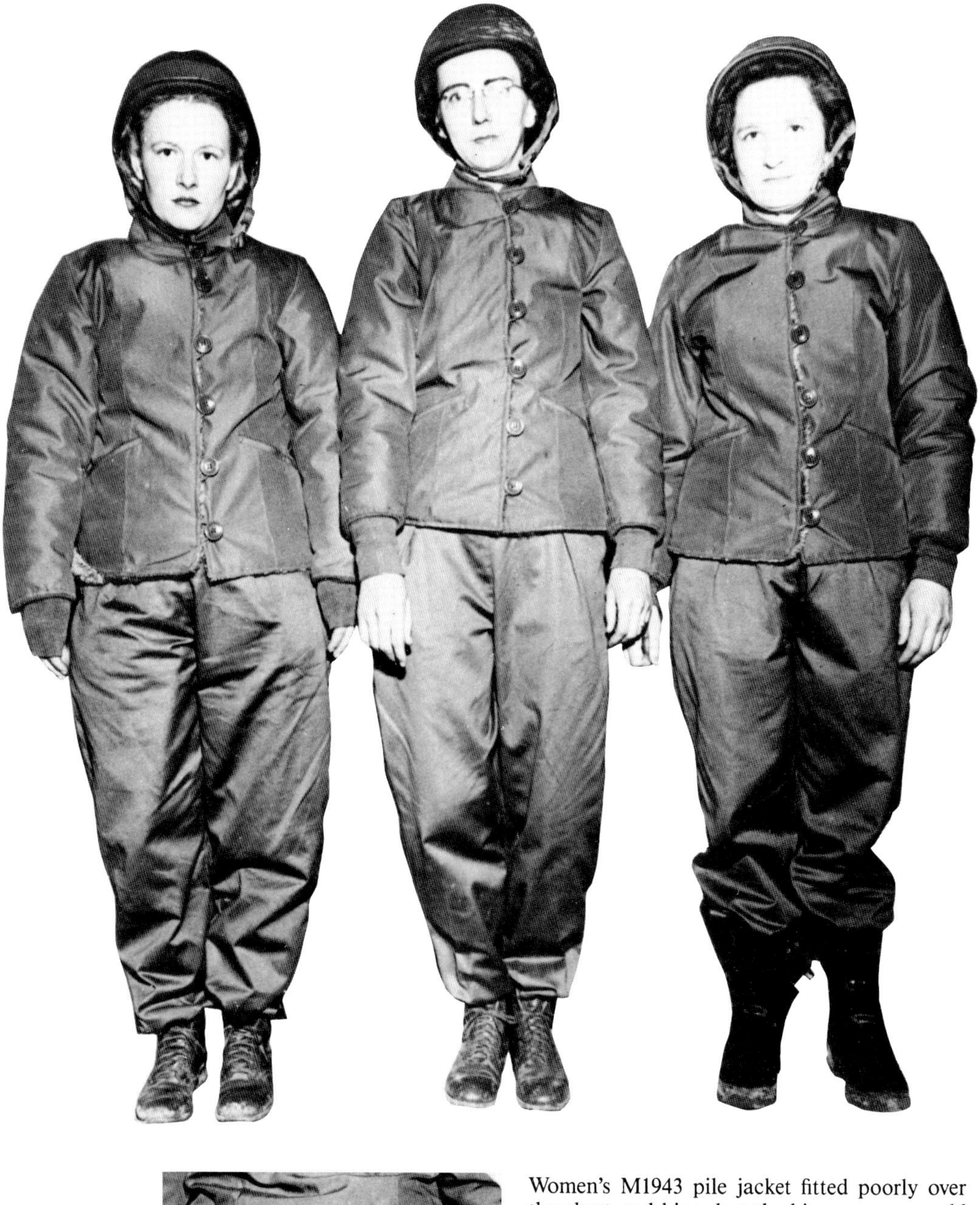

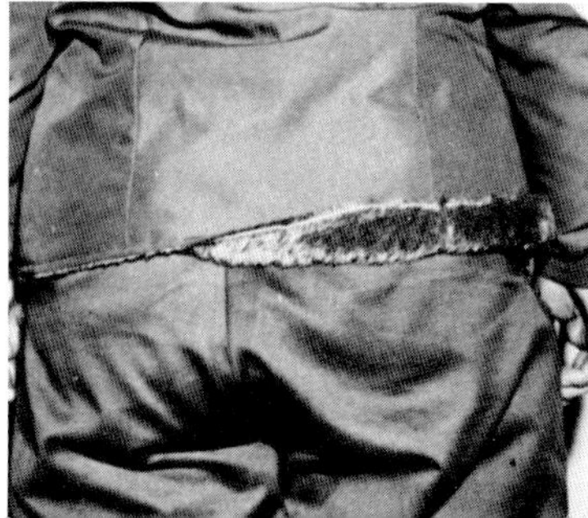

Women's M1943 pile jacket fitted poorly over the chest and hips, but the hip snugness could be eliminated only by issuing a jacket too large in the chest. Note the curling of the pile on the jacket hem, shown in the photograph at left.

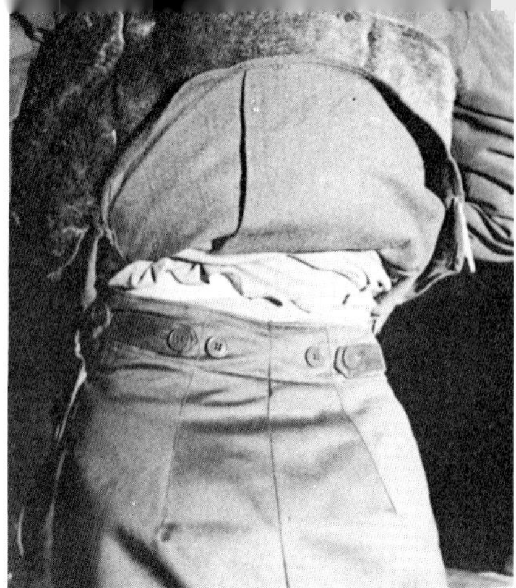

Working in the women's M1943 pile jacket often caused garments worn underneath to distort uncomfortably, such as the back of this sweater, shown when the jacket and wool shirtwaist were pulled up at back. This view also shows the rear buttons on the women's outer cover trousers.

The women's parka-type overcoat, also known as the nurse cold-climate parka-type overcoat, was a single-breasted, alpaca-lined, wind-resistant cotton overcoat with a storm fly that closed with snap fasteners and five buttons.

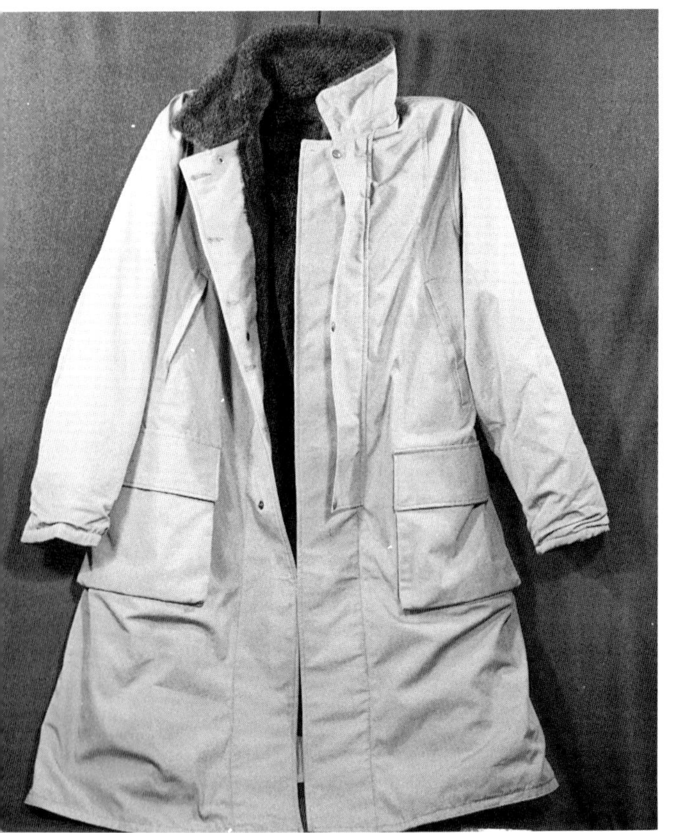

The women's parka-type overcoat shown from the back, with detachable alpaca-lined hood attached to collar (note loose drawstrings ordinarily used for closing hood around face) and the removable web belt at waistline.

Nurses dressed in the women's parka-type overcoat: note the tendency of the snap fasteners to pull out of the material, a failure that could not be readily repaired. Note also the inadequacy of the front closure's buttoning device; the small buttons required a longer shank to accommodate the thick material.

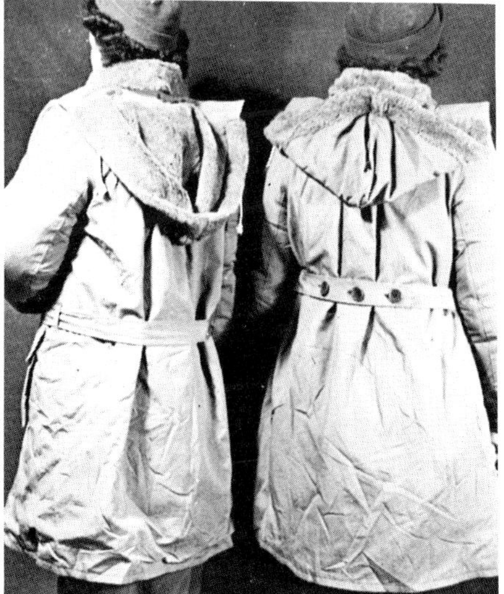

The women's parka-type overcoat, individualized to enhance appearance at Fort Devens during March 1944 *(right)*, compared to standard overcoat *(left)*. The modified overcoat added a three-button half-belt to eliminate the unattractive low waistline effect of the regular belt, and placed another button to keep the hood better secured when not in use.

The alpaca-lined women's parka-type overcoat was a single-breasted overcoat that could be worn for field duty or dress. However, access to the front patch pockets was hindered if auxiliary equipment was worn. The closure snaps did not extend low enough on the coat, and this allowed the flaps to open, which reduced the overcoat's warmth and protective qualities.

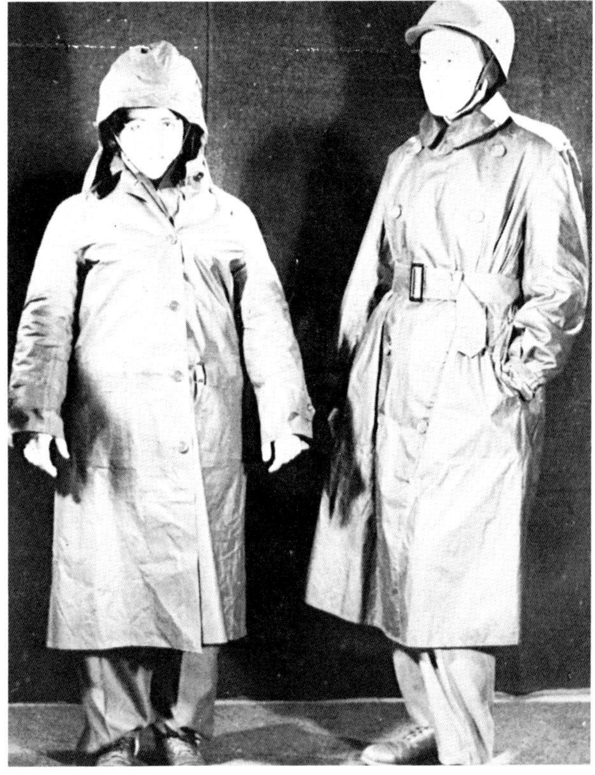

The women's parka-type raincoat *(left)* compared to the regular officer's raincoat *(right)*; the latter was preferred because of its superior style and appearance. The parka-type raincoat collected perspiration inside whenever worn closed during marching, and retained the excessive moisture.

Advance oversea party of Women's Army Auxiliary Corps personnel docking in Scotland during May 1943, wearing women's officer's field overcoats with shoulder straps as well as auxiliary equipment and blanket rolls. Note angle-head flashlight clipped on pistol belt.

The M1941 wool knit toque was a close-fitting hood for head protection in cold weather.

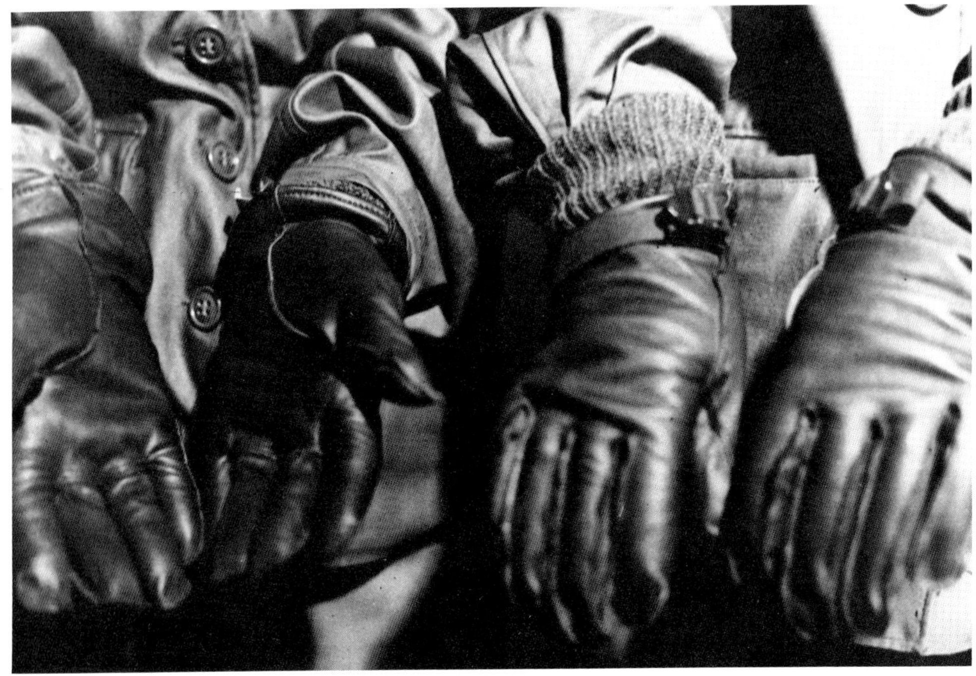

Women's leather glove shells worn over wool glove inserts, showing the wrinkling and bulk of gloves when worn in combination.

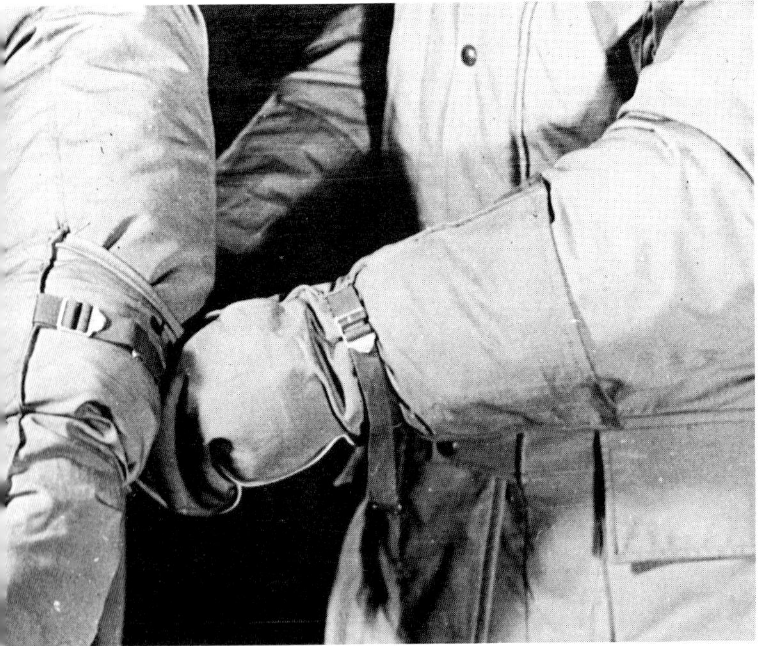

Women's trigger-finger mitten shells were gauntlet styled but required a wider cuff when worn with the field jacket, especially whenever fitted over other layers such as the sweater and pile liner. The Quartermaster General recommended lowering the adjusting strap and added another cuff gusset, as shown here, but such expedients were difficult in the field.

# 7

# Miscellaneous Clothing

The army entered World War II with a relatively large supply of stockinette-type M1 service gas masks, first standardized in 1921 with improved versions in 1934 (M1A1) and 1935 (M1A2). The mask featured a rubberized facepiece supplemented with elastic stockinette and was distinguished by its laminated flat-glass round eyepieces. The M1 service gas mask was supplemented by the cheaper M2 training gas mask, and production on the M2 continued until May 1942.

The service gas mask incorporated several adaptations gleaned from World War I gas warfare experience, but was considered dangerously vulnerable to 1940-era operating conditions. The mouthpiece was linked by hose tubing into a primitive flow-type filter canister that depended on charcoal and soda lime absorbents to purify incoming air. The mask itself was flawed by its vulnerable chin seam, angle tube, separate deflectors (to discharge air over the eyepieces and prevent lens fogging), and numerous metal parts in the eyepiece assembly. The M1-series service gas masks, however, remained in service until 26 October 1944, although they were increasingly relegated to stateside and reserve use during the course of the conflict.

Late in 1940 an improved service gas mask was introduced with a fully molded rubber face-blank that eliminated many of the M1 facepiece problems. Known as the heavyweight service gas mask, the newer model was ready for mass production in June 1941. The mask was judged unsatisfactory for combat conditions during the North African campaign because it was too bulky and uncomfortable, weighed over five pounds, and required a steel-box canister. All gas masks subjected to the tropical climate of the Pacific theater suffered extensive rust and corrosion damage. Approximately 10,500,000 heavyweight masks were procured by the Chemical Warfare Service before production finally ceased in 1943.

The service mask was part of every soldier's equipment, and the need for a functional mask capable of meaningful combat employment was urgently needed. On 29 September 1942, the M3-10-6 lightweight service gas mask was standardized and entered regular production during January 1943. The mask weighed three and a half pounds and was attached to a smaller, rounded M10 canister equipped with enhanced filters and absorbent material. That August the assembly was fitted with a revised facepiece with its distinctive nose cup. The lightweight masks arrived in Europe late in the year, and the old heavyweight masks were exchanged as quickly as possible, although they were kept for parts and as a secondary reserve.

The other lightweight gas mask type was the M4-10A1-6, originally envisioned as an impromptu item while industry resolved teething problems with initial M3 mask production. The M4 was simply constructed by adding the nose cup, hose tube, canister, and carrier of a lightweight mask to a reconditioned heavyweight or M2 rubber facepiece. In spite of its improvised origin, the M4 became an important component of the army's mask turnout and first entered real production at the beginning of 1944. Approximately 13,000,000 masks of both M3 and M4 types were acquired from 1943 through 1945, making the lightweight gas mask the mainstay of army protective equipment.

The lightweight service gas masks initially used an M9 canister that employed a mixture of soda lime and copper-impregnated activated charcoal capable of removing several known gases. Unfortunately, the canister provided very limited protection against hydrogen cyanide and cyanogen chloride. By July 1943 the development of better impregnated charcoals enabled these deficiencies to be resolved in the improved M10 canister. Beginning in 1942, asbestos filters replaced earlier carbon-impregnated filter paper, an air-flow "improvement" that unknowingly presented great health hazards. Following the invasion of North Africa, chemically treated paper fiber, manufactured from Moroccan esparto grass, was substituted for the asbestos product.

The search for a less cumbersome mask assembly, started in June 1943, evolved into the assault gas mask that entered production during February 1944. The mask was fitted with a cheek-mounted M11 aluminum drum auxiliary-flow canister—copied from a German design—and featured a water-repellent smoke filter and deep bed of charcoal. The assembled units weighed three pounds and were first used in regular combat during the D-Day invasion of Normandy. All assault forces wore antigas protective clothing and carried assault gas masks during the landings because the Allies feared that the Germans would initiate gas attacks to defeat the invasion.

A month later, on 7 July 1944, the mask was standardized as the M5-11-7 combat service gas mask. The mask carrier was made of butyl rubber-coated cotton duck carrier that made a waterproof package for the entire assembly. As an emergency flotation device, the carrier saved numerous soldiers from drowning in assault landings. Approximately 520,000 combat service gas masks were obtained before production stopped on the M5 in September 1944.

The utility of the M5 mask was thwarted by both manufacturing difficulties and inherent composition flaws. Rubber shortages mandated use of neoprene in all gas-mask construction after November 1943, and these "black rubber masks" (both M3 and successor M5 models) suffered from several serious defects. The batches of neoprene compound not only lacked uniformity, but had a tendency to "cold set" and deform into unusable shapes during cold weather. This unfortunate condition was not realized until the final European winter campaign, where soldiers found that the stiffened masks were no longer gas-tight.

The unsuitability of the neoprene M5 version forced the army to abandon its promising assault gas-mask design and return to reliance on the lightweight gas-mask models that industry was already geared to produce. The successor model to the M5, the snout-type M8-11-10 (with the assault drum canister attached directly to the front of a reconditioned rubber facepiece) did not enter production until the summer of 1945 and never reached the Pacific theater in appreciable quantity. The army also produced an improved optical gas mask, standardized in January 1944, that contained a diaphragm for speech transmission and small circular lenses for use with binoculars or other instruments. The armored branch considered the mask unsatisfactory, but a newer speech model was not developed before the end of the war.

The Chemical Warfare Service also adopted eye shields for use in case low-flying enemy aircraft sprayed liquid mustard or other vesicant agents. The M1 eye shield, standardized on 23 April 1943, was composed of felt-rimmed cellulose acetate eyepieces mounted on an elastic head strap. On 2 August 1945 the improved M2 eye shield was standardized. The latter model came in both clear and green-tinted acetate, had antifogging ventilation holes in the upper eyepiece corners, and could either fit over spectacles or be folded for pocket carrying. More than 71,928,000 eye shields were procured by the Chemical Warfare Service during the war, with the greatest number (more than 38,203,000) obtained during 1944.

The individual protective cover was adopted from the existing British cape and designed to protect the soldier from liquid vesicants and blistering gases delivered by aerial spray. The cover's tear-tape device enabled it to be put on speedily. The covers were issued on a general basis after October 1942 and 32,891,000 were procured by the army through 1945. The expendable cape was a large cellophane bag that folded into a small packet 4 inches by 7½ inches. The cold-climate individual protective cover, introduced in 1944, was similar but treated to resist cracking during wintry conditions. About 1,512,000 covers were acquired before the war ended. All covers were designed to completely envelop the soldier quickly in an umbrella fashion, but its bulk and manner of wear prevented mobility.

The army's protective combat clothing was effective against both mustard vapor and fine mustard spray, and consisted of two-piece male and female herringbone twill outfits impregnated with the highly secretive chloroamide cloth impregnite known as the CC-2 solution. In addition to these basic outer garments, a double layer of long or short underwear, gloves, socks, leggings, and hood was necessary for complete protection. The most common item of this double-layer set was the impregnated woolen hood, a standard quartermaster item, worn over the gas mask to protect the head and neck from vesicant gases.

In addition to gas masks, combat footgear also presented the army with formidable design and production problems during the war. At the outset of the national emergency the Quartermaster Corps was more concerned with replacing the high-top garrison shoe with an economical low-quarter shoe than with developing versatile combat footwear. However, during the 1940 maneuvers the Type I light service shoes wore through with such alarming rapidity that the development of better shoes demanded immediate attention.

The search for durability led to the development of composition soles in 1940, but this effort was hindered by sudden restrictions placed on vital raw materials. The rubber shortage eroded the quality of the once-promising Type II service shoe, which incorporated a rubber tap heel. Eventually the taps were made entirely of inferior reclaimed rubber of no lasting value. By 1942 efforts to conserve materials such as leather, duck, rubber, and brass led to a considerably lowered shoe quality. The sturdiness of footwear deteriorated as wood core heels, cork filler, strip gumming, zinc-coated nails, and thinner insoles became accepted substitutes in footwear manufacture. By mid-1942 the army was forced to reappraise the wisdom of such manufacturing shortcuts.

Another factor in the army's reappraisal of its footwear program was the universal dislike by soldiers of the basic service shoe and leggings combination. Troops complained about the inconvenience of donning and taking off leggings, their lack of durability, the easily broken laces, and the complicated lacing configurations. Because changing shoes and leggings was so involved, many soldiers chose not to do so on a regular basis, which increased the chance of ankle and foot afflictions. As a result, the Quartermaster Corps began researching the practicality of a combat boot.

The first combat boot design was produced in conjunction with Desert Training Center efforts to form specialized desert units. The desert boot was a three-quarter-length buckle boot with a duck top that was soon being developed alongside the Quartermaster Project T-152 field boot, which formed part of the M1943 experimental combat outfit. In conformity with General Marshall's desires to convert specialty gear to general wartime application, these prototype desert and field combat boots were reconsidered for general purpose, army-wide application. A style of heavy-duty shoe with top cuff and strap, copied from the

Canadian combat boot, was subsequently favored. On 1 February 1943 General Marshall gave final authority for the army to adopt the boot design because light service shoes proved unsuitable for battlefield use.

The quartermaster sample that General Marshall received on 5 February 1943 became available as the Type III shoe that April. The upper was made of leather that was durable, could absorb more dubbing for better waterproofing, and was comfortable even when being broken in. The rubber sole and heel were later made of reclaimed and finally synthetic rubber. A combat boot version was produced by simply adding a cuff and buckle top that extended the height by 4 inches (to 10 inches), which allowed for the elimination of the despised leggings. The combat boot was selected to replace the Type III shoe in July, became standardized on 16 November 1943, and went into production as a regular item of issue to all soldiers during January 1944.

The ordinary combat boot, however, did not protect soldiers from trenchfoot and other foot ailments caused by prolonged exposure to cold mud and icy slush. Leather is a permeable material and leaking around the seams was impossible to check with applications of dubbing. If these applications were sufficient to stop leaking, then the dubbing inhibited rapid drying when the leather got wet. Rubber overshoes, arctic overshoes, and shoe pacs were recommended for protection in inclement weather conditions.

Shoe pacs were made of moccasin style rubber bottoms topped with leather and were usually worn with wool ski socks. The shoe pacs were more waterproof than either shoes or boots, but the soles tended to wear quickly and foot support was minimal. Following heavy foot injuries among army troops wearing 12-inch Blucher boots in the Aleutian campaign, the army adopted shoe pacs as preferred winter footwear. The first requisition for shoe pacs in the European theater was placed as early as mid-August 1944, but most divisions did not receive their initial shoe pacs until late January 1945.

Overshoes and shoe pacs did not provide a totally satisfactory answer to the need for foot protection in cold and wet weather fighting. The overshoes were made from inferior rubber. The shoe pacs also had numerous weaknesses, including a tendency for the stitching to pull apart where the rubber foot was connected to the leather upper. Arch supports and raised heels offered better support in later shoe pac models but were often lacking in issues made during the height of the European winter campaign. Even more serious, many soldiers experienced cold-weather injuries to their feet when wearing insulated shoe pacs because their feet perspired excessively and the moisture froze when the soldiers stopped moving.

The army's early wartime experience with jungle footwear stemmed from Capt. Cresson H. Kearny's experimental platoons in Panama. He demonstrated that leather service shoes deteriorated rapidly in wet-torrid climates and that specialized footwear was required. Following extensive development, a sneaker-type canvas jungle boot, with a corrugated rubber sole and permeable duck upper, was standardized for tropical warfare at the end of August 1942. Unfortunately, difficulties in securing crude or reclaimed rubber for canvas footwear, as well as difficulties in efficient production, prevented widespread use of the jungle boot until mid-1943. When the boots were worn in combat, it was soon discovered that the boots fit poorly, were too fragile for sustained use, and offered little arch or foot support. Also, the canvas upper caused so much discomfort from chafing that troops either turned down the tops or cut them off.

A new lightweight jungle boot was designed during 1944. This boot featured a spun-nylon duck upper, treated for mildew prevention, that fastened with two straps and a buckle. The boot had a leather mid-sole as well as a cleated rubber outer sole and heel. The improved tropical combat boot was standardized in November 1944, despite lingering problems with connecting the boot uppers to the sole portion. Mass production, however, did not start until the summer of 1945, by which time operations were no longer concentrated within jungle regions of the Pacific theater. The cessation of hostilities at the end of August terminated further tropical boot contracts.

# Protective Clothing and Equipment

Basic soldiering protection against toxic agents was provided by the gas mask connected to a breathing filtration canister. The masks were designed to protect individuals against toxic agents such as phosgene and mustard gas. The army fortunately never confronted German nerve gases, which remained unknown to Allied intelligence until after the war. This infantryman wears the training gas mask with field equipment during 1940.

The M1A2 service gas mask worn with sectional tent-poncho during 1943 chemical warfare testing. Lens placement on the early mask eyepieces hampered the soldier's field of vision and created dead air space within the mask. More seriously, any mask worn without the protective hood exposed the wearer to serious blistering injuries, since the neck was one of the two body areas most vulnerable to the effects of mustard gas.

Soldier's permeable protective clothing in mid-1943: (1) protective wool hood, (2) M4 service gas mask, (3) one-piece herringbone twill protective suit (the right sleeve has same impregnation type as suit body and left sleeve is impregnated differently for mustard spray tests), (4) protective cotton gloves, (5) protective dismounted canvas leggings, (6) impregnated service shoes.

Female medical personnel wearing the M3 lightweight gas mask and protective clothing during testing at Fort Oglethorpe, Georgia, in October 1943. The medical aid person *(left)* is donning the protective hood while the driver *(right)* prepares to put on her mask. The large size of the mask carrier is plainly visible.

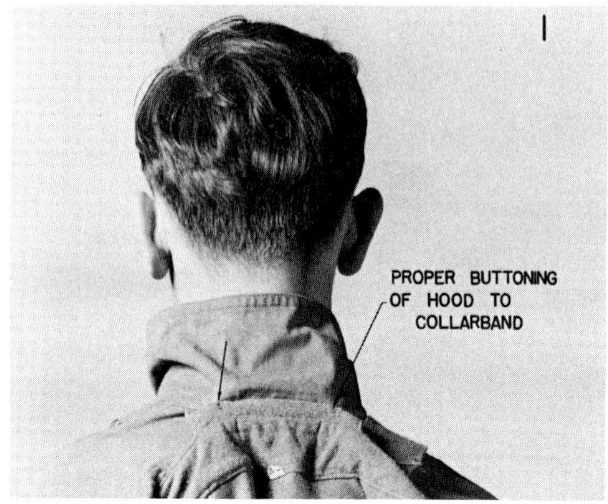


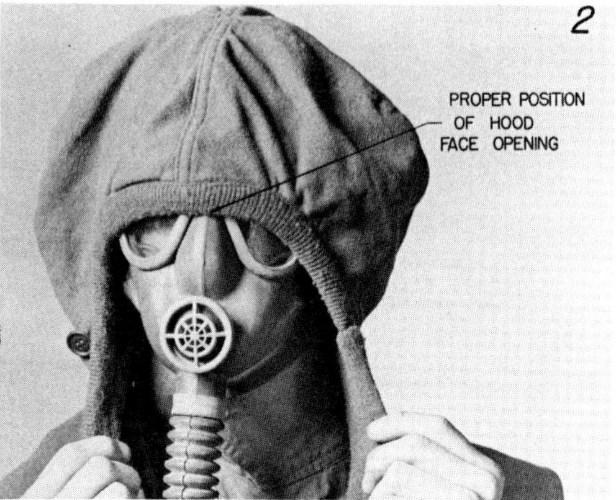


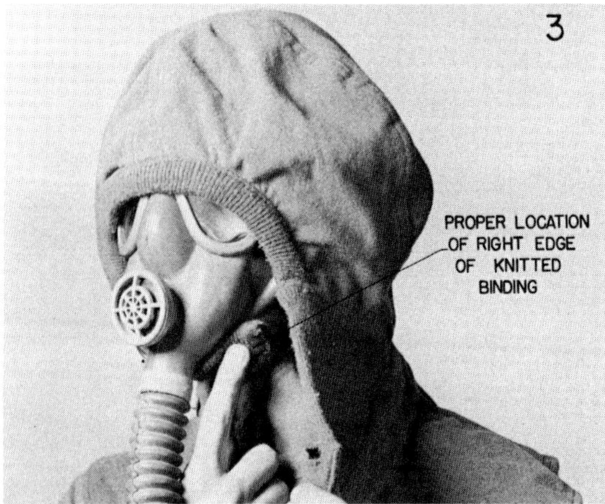


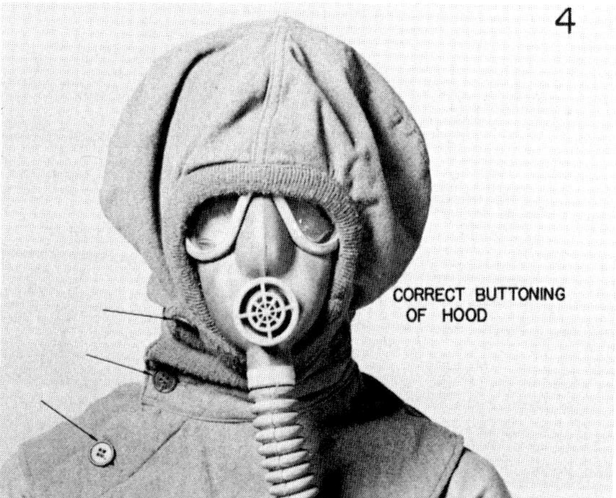


The protective wool hood, designed to prevent vapors from reaching the soldier's head and neck, required eight-step adjustment for the knitted binding to fit snugly against the gas mask.

1. Attach hood by two buttons after upturning collar.
2. Adjust for gas-tightness and pull hood over the head.
3. Place right edge of knitted hood binding underneath chin.
4. Place left binding flap over right edge by fastening buttons.
5. Adjust hood upper binding over the eyepieces.
6. Correctly fit soldier's protective hood.
7. Stretch hood lining if snug fit pulled hood from mask sides.
8. Adjust buttons if fit is not gas-tight (the soldier was expected to accomplish this before an emergency).

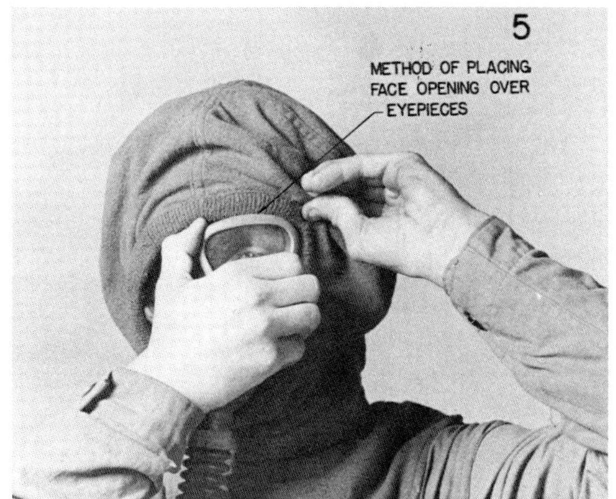
5
METHOD OF PLACING FACE OPENING OVER EYEPIECES

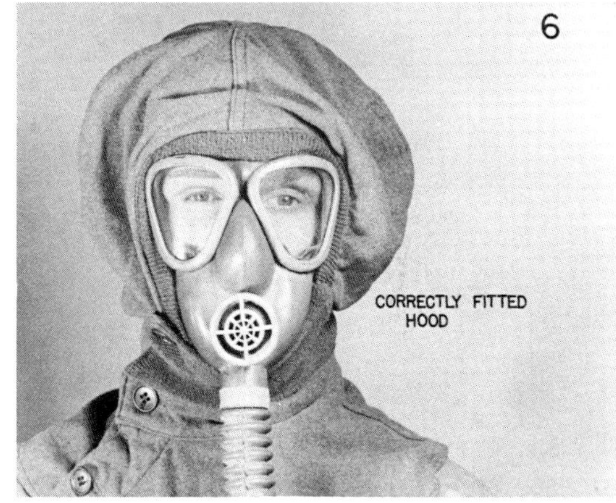
6
CORRECTLY FITTED HOOD

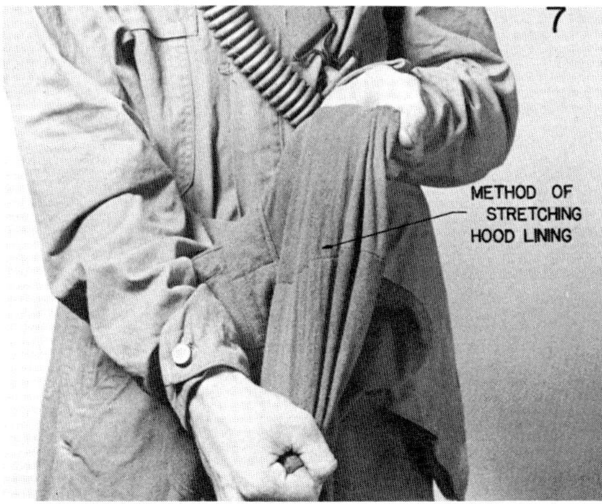
7
METHOD OF STRETCHING HOOD LINING

8
BUTTON A
IMPROPERLY FITTED HOOD. BUTTON A MUST BE RESET

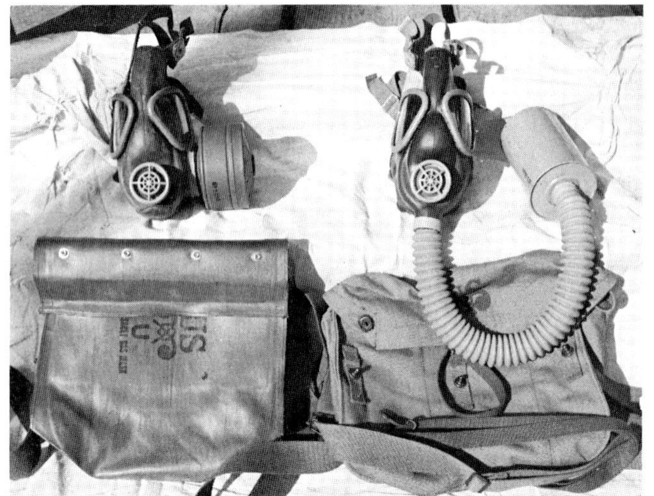

Actual items used for gas countermeasures during D-Day in June 1944 included this drum canister–equipped assault gas mask (*left*, later designated the M5 combat service gas mask) with its waterproof carrier. It is contrasted with the M3 lightweight service gas mask and M10 canister *(right)*, connected by the awkward hose that interfered with prone firing. Unfortunately, both neoprene "black rubber mask" types proved defective under winter fighting conditions.

Actual D-Day assault clothing, consisting of herringbone twill field trousers and jacket (along with cap, socks, and shorts) impregnated with CC-2 chloroamide. This treated clothing set was worn with untreated flannel shirt and wool trousers. Note protective ointment kit containing tubes of M5 chlorine compound ointments and a British antilewiste eye ointment.

Marine protective clothing worn by selected naval demolition and army amphibian engineer personnel during the Normandy invasion of June 1944.

Army soldier in complete individual protective outfit during aerial-delivered mustard gas testing during June 1943: (1) transparent window, (2) impermeable sleeves, pulled down to show length and upper ends, (3) forearm protection, (4) panels to record Chemical Warfare Service spray results, (5) impermeable mittens, (6) impermeable individual protective cover.

The women's special protective herringbone twill shirt and trousers, impregnated with the secret CC-2 chloroamide, during chemical testing at Fort Oglethorpe, Georgia, in September 1943. Note that the large sleeves had to be pinned for adequate gas protection.

The women's special protective herringbone twill shirt and trousers with hood, showing fit of the protective clothing from the side. Note disproportionate fullness of the shirt, which caused bulkiness at waist and hindered tight antigas sealing.

# Footwear

The M1943 composition-sole service shoes, with an outside tap of reclaimed rubber, are worn with M1938 first-pattern leggings with two eyelets per hook, a design discarded during the course of the war to conserve brass fittings. Soldiers disliked leggings because they soaked up water, chafed the legs, and took too long to put on. Note M1916 holster with tie-down thong laced through eyelets. Also note wartime censor markings on photograph.

*(Right)* The experimental M1943 field boot, a high-topped boot with uppers of reversed leather, was enthusiastically received by infantrymen during combat tests in both North Africa and Italy. Unfortunately, the soft-tanning process caused the leather to shrink when wet and its reverse construction absorbed water readily. These defects went uncorrected when the combat service boot was standardized.

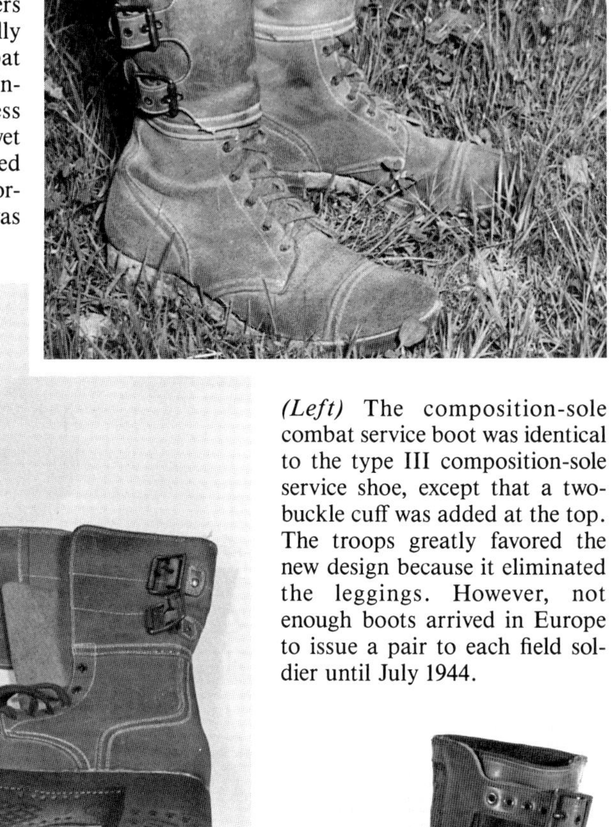

*(Left)* The composition-sole combat service boot was identical to the type III composition-sole service shoe, except that a two-buckle cuff was added at the top. The troops greatly favored the new design because it eliminated the leggings. However, not enough boots arrived in Europe to issue a pair to each field soldier until July 1944.

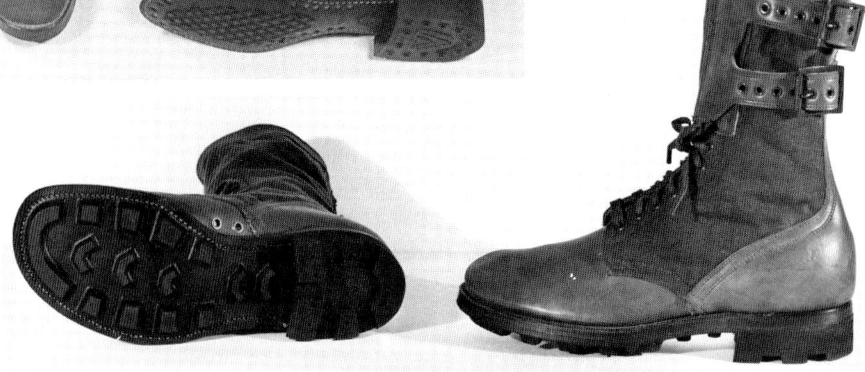

The tropical combat boot replaced the cotton jungle boot, and was designed to fit comfortably and give protective support to the ankle and foot in jungle territories. The narrow spacing between the rubber cleats of the soles and heels muddied easily, however, and its 1944 development placed it in the field too late to benefit operations in jungle terrain.

The parachute jumper boot, a 10-inch combat service boot with a rubber tap and rubber heel, was designed to give maximum ankle protection.

Paratroopers of the 511th Parachute Inf regiment with their parachute jumper boots, cherished even in a tropical environment for their superior wear and sturdy design.

Arctic felt snowshoes were highly satisfactory footwear that combined a superior-quality felt sole with thin leather outer sole. The design was later extended into an arctic felt boot.

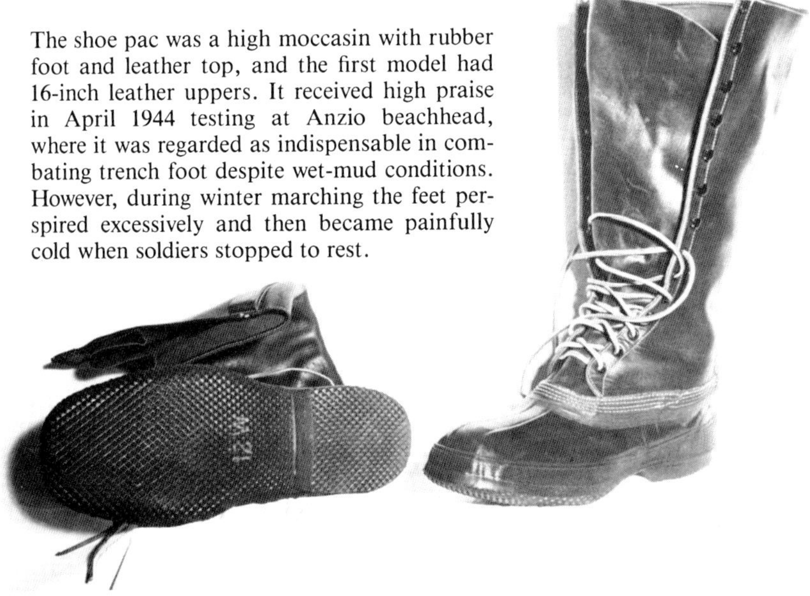

The shoe pac was a high moccasin with rubber foot and leather top, and the first model had 16-inch leather uppers. It received high praise in April 1944 testing at Anzio beachhead, where it was regarded as indispensable in combating trench foot despite wet-mud conditions. However, during winter marching the feet perspired excessively and then became painfully cold when soldiers stopped to rest.

The M1944 shoe pac had a 12-inch upper, a steel shank, and a more waterproof seam between the leather and rubber. The shoe pac was designed to accommodate two pairs of wool ski socks and one pair of felt insoles, but its frequent misuse as a marching boot caused serious foot problems during the 1944 Ardennes campaign.

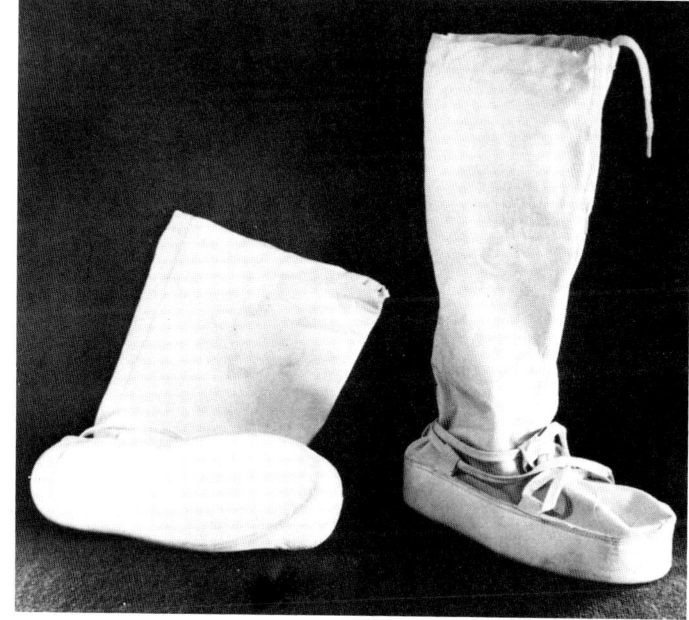

The mukluk boot was the warmest footwear issued for extreme cold and dry snow conditions. It was designed as a permeable boot to allow evaporation of foot perspiration, and thus absorbed water quickly and became worthless in wet snow or in temperatures above 20 degrees Fahrenheit. The mukluk was unsuitable for use around vehicles, because its soft fabric top and kidskin or buckskin bottoms lost shape and gave scant protection.

# U.S. ARMY UNIFORM MAP OF THE ZONE OF INTERIOR

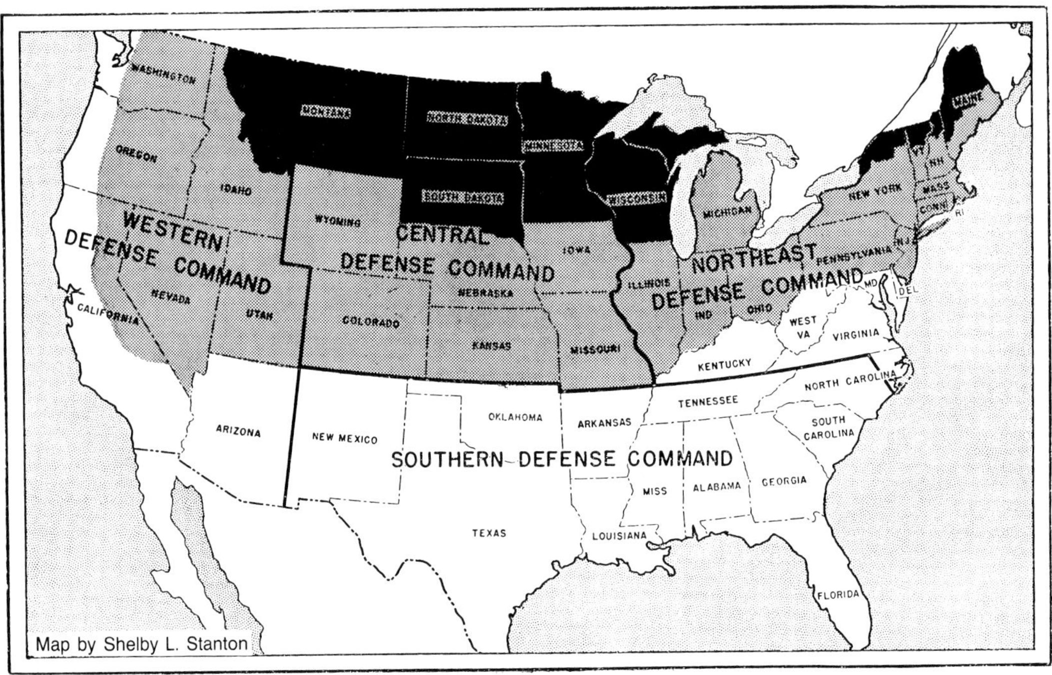


U.S. Zone of Interior, with defense command boundaries adopted 17 March 1941, showing temperate zone 1 (black), zone 2 (gray), and zone 3 (plain). Zone 1, also known as the cold zone, included states shown and Michigan's Upper Peninsula, as well as New York's Jefferson, St. Lawrence, Franklin, and Clinton counties; Maine's Aroostook, Piscataquis, Somerset, Penobscot, Oxford, and Franklin counties; New Hampshire's Coos County; and Vermont's Franklin, Orleans, Essex, Washington, Lamoille, Grande Isle, Caledonia, and Chittenden counties. Zone 2 included areas in and east of the Cascade Range and Sierra Nevadas of Washington, Oregon, and California.

# U.S. ARMY UNIFORM MAP OF THE WORLD

*Map appears on following pages*

## Troop Stationing and Uniform Issue Areas: 1 January 1943

**1** Australia
**2** Guadalcanal
**3** Espiritu Santo
**4** New Caledonia
**5** Efate
**6** Fiji
**7** New Zealand
**8** Tongatabu
**9** Aitutaki
**10** Bora Bora
**11** Tongareva
**12** Canton
**13** Fanning
**14** Christmas
**15** Hawaii
**16** Alaska
**17** Western Canada
**18** Eastern Canada
**19** Western Defense Command
**20** Central Defense Command
**21** Southern Defense Command
**22** Eastern Defense Command
**23** Cuba
**24** Guatemala
**25** Panama
**26** Galápagos
**27** Bahamas
**28** Jamaica
**29** Aruba
**30** Curaçao
**31** Trinidad
**32** St. Lucia
**33** Antigua
**34** St. Croix
**35** St. Thomas
**36** Puerto Rico
**37** Ecuador
**38** Peru
**39** Chile
**40** Venezuela
**41** British Guiana
**42** Surinam
**43** Brazil
**44** Bermuda
**45** Newfoundland
**46** Greenland
**47** Iceland
**48** United Kingdom
**49** Morocco-Algeria-Tunisia
**50** Liberia
**51** Ascension
**52** Gold Coast
**53** Central Africa
**54** Delta Service Command
**55** Levant Service Command
**56** Persian Gulf Service Command
**57** Eritrea Service Command
**58** Ramgarh, China-Burma-India

## Clothing distribution key for map appearing on following pages.

White: Arctic, extreme cold
Dotted: Arctic, wet cold*
Shaded: Temperate
Black: Tropics

*Hokkaido Island, tip of Kamchatka Peninsula, Aleutian Islands, extreme southern Alaska, southeastern Alaska, New Brunswick, Nova Scotia, Newfoundland, coastal tip of Greenland, Iceland, coastal Norway to Tromsö.

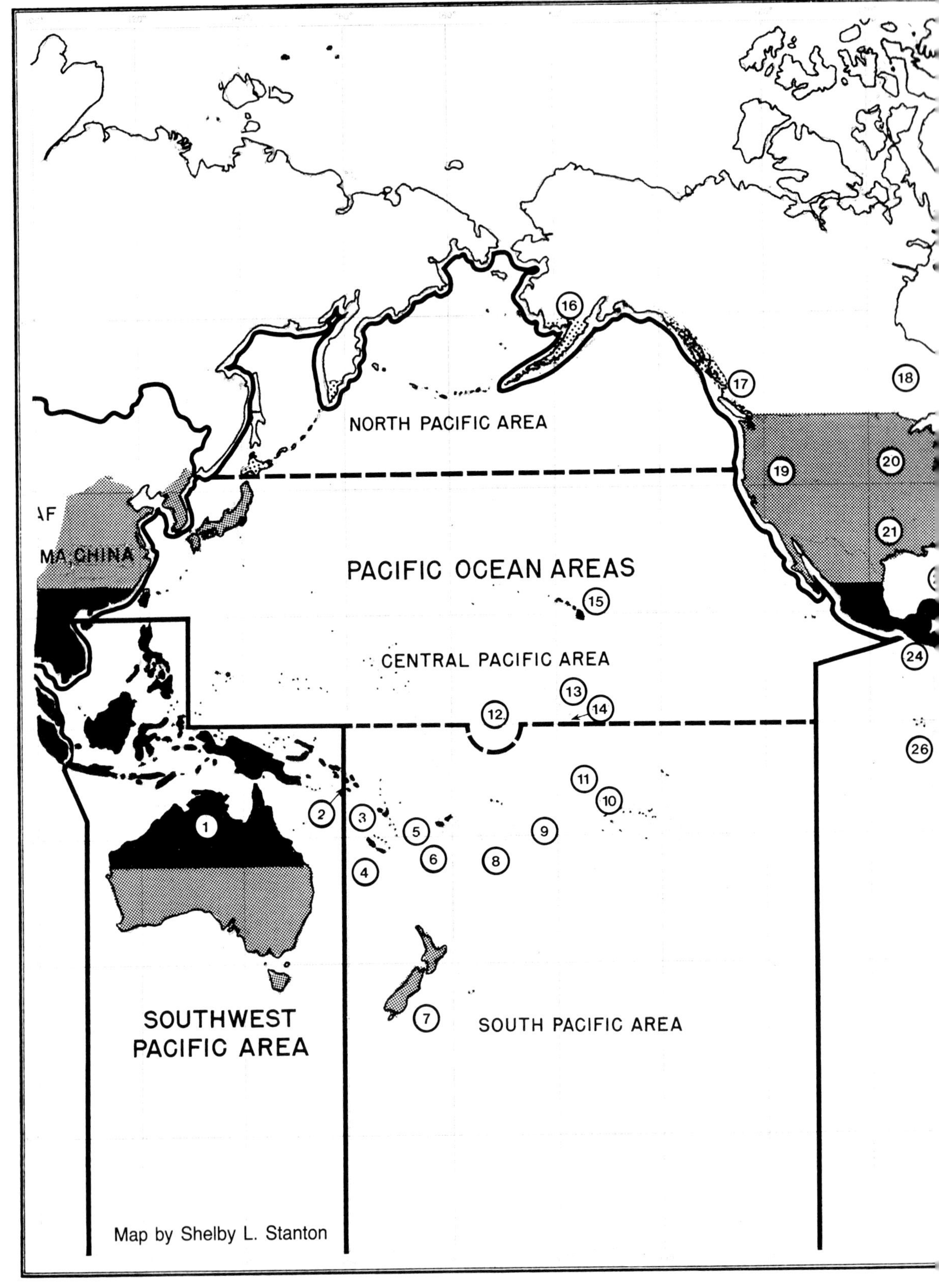

NORTH PACIFIC AREA
PACIFIC OCEAN AREAS
CENTRAL PACIFIC AREA
SOUTH PACIFIC AREA
SOUTHWEST
PACIFIC AREA
AF
MA,CHINA
1
2
3
4
5
6
7
8
9
10
11
12
13
14
15
16
17
18
19
20
21
24
26
Map by Shelby L. Stanton

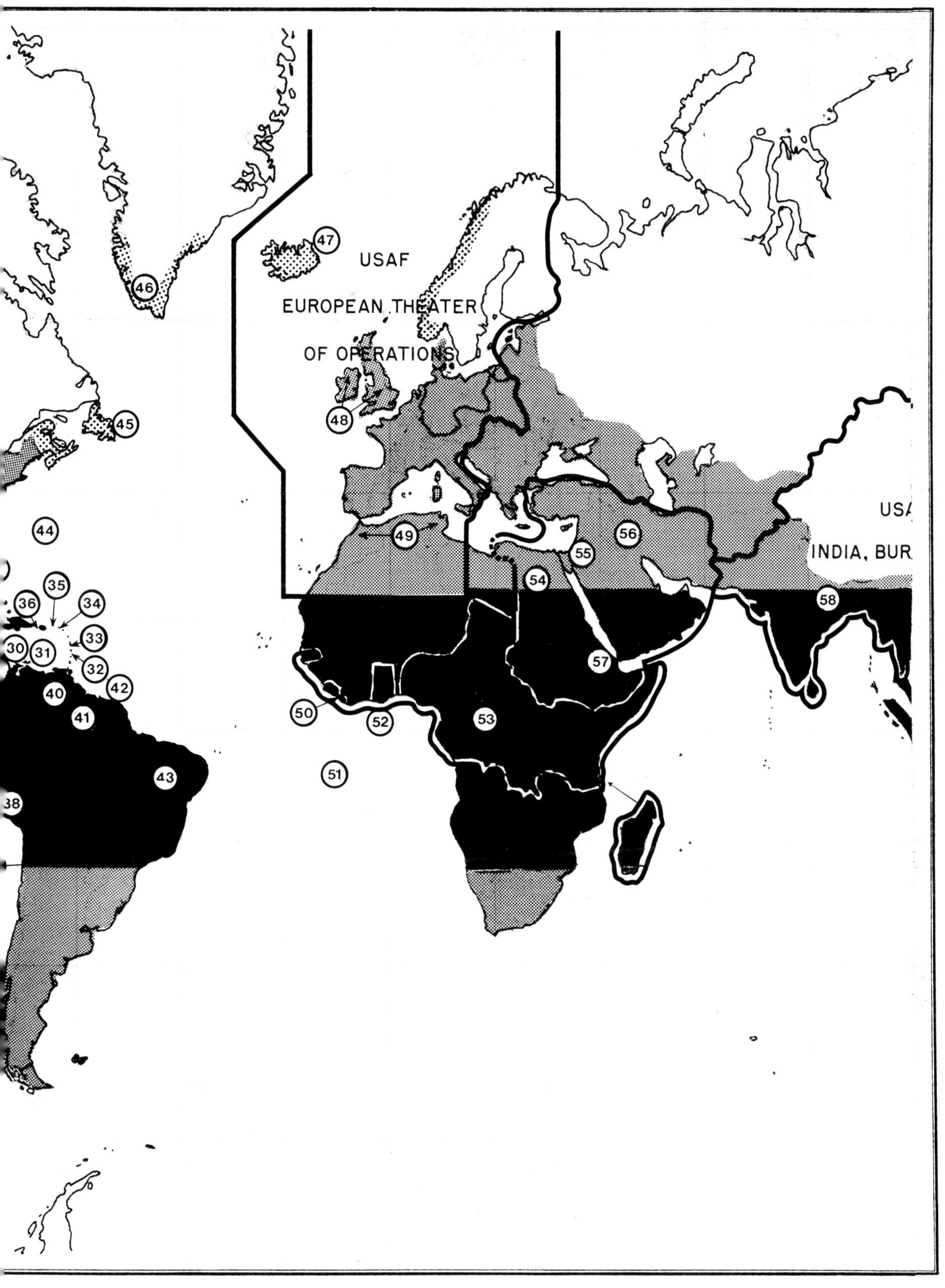

USAF
EUROPEAN THEATER
OF OPERATIONS
USA
INDIA, BUR
30
31
32
33
34
35
36
38
40
41
42
43
44
45
46
47
48
49
50
51
52
53
54
55
56
57
58

# APPENDIX A

## Clothing and Individual Equipment Allowances

Clothing and individual equipment allowances during World War II depended on organization, assignment or activity, and climatic area or zone. The most common documents governing supply were the War Department Tables of Organization and Equipment (T/O&E) and Tables of Equipment (T/E) 21.

**T/O & E 6–125**

FA BATTALION, MOTORIZED, 155-MM GUN, SELF-PROPELLED

ORDNANCE

*Weapons and miscellaneous*

| 1 | 2 | 3 | 4 |
|---|---|---|---|
| Item | Allowances | For computation | Basis of distribution and remarks |
| Watch, wrist, 7-jewel | 2 | ------ | |
| *Vehicles* | | | |
| Trailer, ¼-ton, 2-wheel, cargo | 1 | ------ | |
| Truck: | | | |
| ¼-ton, 4 x 4 | 1 | ------ | |
| ¾-ton, weapons carrier, w/winch. | 1 | ------ | |
| *Motor transport equipment* | | | |
| Axe, handled, chopping, single-bit, standard grade, weight, 4-pound. | 2 | ------ | 1 per trk. |
| Defroster and Deicer, electric, windshield. | 2 | ------ | 1 per trk when atzd by army or T of Opns comdr. |
| Mattock, handled, pick, Type II, Class F, 5-pound. | 1 | ------ | Per trk, ¾-ton. |
| Rope, tow, 20-ft. by 1-in diameter. | 2 | ------ | 1 per trk. |
| Shovel, general purpose, D-handled, strap-back, round-point, No. 2. | 2 | ------ | Do. |

QUARTERMASTER

*Individual equipment*

| Item | Allowances | For computation | Basis of distribution and remarks |
|---|---|---|---|
| Bag, canvas, field, od, M1936 | 12 | ------ | 1 per indiv (except in Alaska). |
| Belt, pistol or revolver, M1936 | 12 | ------ | 1 per indiv. |
| Cover, canteen, dismounted, M1910. | 12 | ------ | Do. |
| Strap, carrying, od, bag, canvas, field | 12 | ------ | 1 per bag, canvas, fld. od, M1936. |
| Suspenders, belt, M1936 | 12 | ------ | Do. |

Sample page from T/O&E no. 6-125, effective 29 September 1943, showing additional quartermaster items specifically allocated to a self-propelled 155mm gun motorized field artillery battalion at this stage of the war.

20 CLOTHING AND INDIVIDUAL EQUIPMENT

*ENLISTED WOMAN, WOMEN'S ARMY CORPS, BY OCCUPATION*

(Allowances in this section are in addition to allowances in preceding section)

*MANDATORY ALLOWANCES*

| 1 | 2 | | | | | | | | 3 |
|---|---|---|---|---|---|---|---|---|---|
| Item | Allowances | | | | | | | | Basis of issue and remarks |
| | Baker | Cook | Military police | Indoor worker (see part IV, sec III) | Outdoor worker (see part IV, sec III) | Airplane mechanic (see part IV, sec III) | Enlisted women on recruiting duty | Enlisted women on duty in hospital and dental clinics | |
| *Individual clothing* | | | | | | | | | |
| Bandanna, women's ea | | | | | | 2 | | | |
| Cap, herringbone twill ea | | | | 1 | 1 | | | | |
| Dress, WAC, hospital ea | | | | | | | | 9 | |
| Glove-inserts, wool, women's pr | | | | | 2 | | | | In Z 2 and 3 only. |
| Glove-shells, leather, women's pr | | | | | 1 | | | | Do. |
| Gloves: | | | | | | | | | |
| Leather, dress, women's pr | | | | | | | 1 | | |
| WAC, work, cotton pr | 1 | 1 | | | 1 | | | | |
| Hood, jacket, field, M-1943, women's ea | | | | | 1 | | | | Auth only when jacket, fld, M1943 is issued. |
| Jacket: | | | | | | | | | |
| Field, M-1943, women's ea | | | | | 1 | | | | In Z 2 and 3 only. |
| WAC: | | | | | | | | | |
| Summer, tropical, worsted, khaki ea | | | | | | | 2 | | |
| Winter ea | | | | | | | 1 | | |
| Leggings, canvas, women's pr | | | | | 2 | | | | Do. |
| Liner, jacket, field, M-1943, women's ea | | | | | 1 | | | | Do. |
| Overcoat, women's, parka type ea | | | | | 1 | | | | In Z 1 only. |
| Overshoes, Arctic, women's, 4-buckle pr | | | | | 1 | | | | In Z 3 only. |
| Shirt, herringbone twill, women's special. ea | | | | 1 | 1 | | | | |
| Shoes: | | | | | | | | | |
| Field, women's pr | | | | 1 | 1 | | | | |
| Service, women's, low pr | | | | 1 | 1 | | | | |
| Skirt, WAC, winter ea | | | | | | | 1 | | |
| Trousers: | | | | | | | | | |
| Herringbone twill, women's special ea | | | | 1 | 1 | | | | |
| Women's: | | | | | | | | | |
| Outer cover ea | | | | | 1 | | | | Z 2 and 3 only. |
| Wool liner ea | | | | | 1 | | | | Do. |
| *Individual equipment* | | | | | | | | | |
| Brassard, arm, MP ea | | | 1 | | | | | | Perform g patrol dty asgmt. |
| Towel, bath ea | 2 | 2 | | | | | | | |

*DISCRETIONARY ALLOWANCES*

| Item | Baker | Cook | Military police | Indoor worker | Outdoor worker | Airplane mechanic | Recruiting duty | Hospital and dental clinics | Basis of issue and remarks |
|---|---|---|---|---|---|---|---|---|---|
| *When authorized by commanding officer* | | | | | | | | | |
| Apron, WAC, cook's, baker's ea | 6 | 6 | | | | | | | |
| Cap, WAC, cook's, baker's ea | 4 | 4 | | | | | | | |
| Dress, WAC, working, cook's, baker's ea | 6 | 6 | | | | | | | |
| *When authorized by CG service command* | | | | | | | | | |
| Shirt, herringbone twill, women's special. ea | | | | | 1 | | | | For EW with MOS of 345, 747, 754, 932. |
| Trousers, herringbone twill, women's special. ea | | | | | 1 | | | | Do. |

Sample page from T/E no. 21, effective 1 September 1945, part II, section I, subsection C (Enlisted Women), governing mandatory and discretionary issue in the U.S. Zone of Interior. Note that issue of clothing depended on temperate zoning, illustrated in the book's uniform map.

# APPENDIX B

## Theater Tests of the Tropical Uniform

| Test Period | 37th Inf. Div. (OQMG Test 293, Bougainville) Jul–Oct 44 | 7th Inf. Div. (OQMG Test 309A) Oct 44–Feb 45 |
|---|---|---|
| 1. Garments tested | Jacket, poplin*, non-WRT*<br>Jacket, uniform twill*<br>Trousers, poplin, non-WRT<br>Trousers, uniform twill | Jacket, poplin*, WRT*<br>Trousers, poplin, WRT<br>Trousers, uniform twill* |
| 2. Fabric | Poplin preferred to HBT* and uniform twill. Better "feel" smoother and softer than HBT. Recommended for jacket and trousers. | Poplin preferred to HBT and uniform twill. Recommended for jacket and trousers. |
| 3. Durability | Poplin satisfactory for both jacket and trousers. Poplin equal to HBT and uniform twill in four months' wear under combat conditions. | Poplin jacket and trousers outwear HBT. After four months' intermittent wear, 93% jackets and 86% poplin trousers showed little or no wear. |
| 4. Heat load | Poplin cooler than HBT and uniform twill. | Poplin cooler than HBT and uniform twill, particularly after laundering. |
| 5. Dirt penetration | No comment. | Notably less with poplin than with HBT. Mud dries on poplin and can be brushed off, whereas it becomes embedded in HBT. |

| 124th Cavalry Regt. (Sp.) (OQMG Test 309B) Oct 44–Mar 45 | 41st Inf. Div. (OQMG Test 309C) May–Jun 44 |
|---|---|
| Jacket, poplin*, WRT*<br>Trousers, poplin, WRT<br>Trousers, uniform twill* | Jacket, poplin*, WRT*<br>Trousers, poplin, WRT<br>Trousers, uniform twill* |
| Almost 100% of men prefer test garments to HBT. Garments look better, are more comfortable and "creep" less than HBT. Preference for poplin and uniform twill about 50–50. | Poplin preferred to HBT and uniform twill. Recommended for jacket and trousers. |
| Sufficiently durable after six weeks' wear in combat training. Test clothing does not snag or tear as much in undergrowth as HBT. Some stitching failure. | Poplin satisfactory for both jacket and trousers in one month test. Test continuing. |
| Test garments cooler than HBT. Perspiration absorption poor until garments were washed 2–3 times. | Poplin cooler than HBT and uniform twill; became cooler with laundering. |
| No comment. | Notably less with poplin than with HBT, hence less washing required. |

**(continued)**

## Theater Tests of the Tropical Uniform (continued)

| Test Period | 37th Inf. Div. (OQMG Test 293, Bougainville) Jul–Oct 44 | 7th Inf. Div. (OQMG Test 309A) Oct 44–Feb 45 |
|---|---|---|
| **6. Water absorption** | Differs little from HBT and uniform twill. No recommendation on WRT. | Less than that of HBT and uniform twill. Recommend that WRT be eliminated. |
| **7. Launderability** | Satisfactory: washed 20 times using GI soap, scrub brushes, sometimes boiling water. | Poplin easier to wash than HBT or uniform twill. Washed an average of 14 times, usually by natives. |
| **8. Drying time** | Poplin superior to HBT and uniform twill. | Poplin dries rapidly; superior to HBT or uniform twill. |
| **9. Mosquito protection** | Excellent for all fabrics, including HBT. | Few mosquitoes seen, but 82% of the men favored poplin to HBT for mosquito protection. |
| **10. Jacket design** | | |
| a. Shoulder loops | Eliminate. | Eliminate. |
| b. Neck buttons | Eliminate. | No comment. |
| c. CWS flap | Eliminate. | Sew back. |
| d. Pockets | No comment. | Satisfactory. Add pencil slot to left pocket and enclose pistol cover. |
| e. Sleeve design | No comment. | Redesign gusset. |
| f. Jacket length | No comment. | 20% of jackets too long. |
| g. Side vents | No comment. | Retain. |
| h. Button type | Use bone or plastic sewn-on buttons rather than metal tack-on buttons. | Use sewn-on buttons. |

| 124th Cavalry Regt. (Sp.) (OQMG Test 309B) Oct 44–Mar 45 | 41st Inf. Div. (OQMG Test 309C) May–Jun 44 |
|---|---|
| More water resistant than HBT. Lighter than HBT when wet or dry. (Note: True only of poplin.) | Less than that of HBT and uniform twill. Recommended that WRT be eliminated. |
| Hard to get clothing wet enough to wash for first 2–3 washings. Laundered in streams by pounding on flat surface. | Washed only 2–3 times, using GI soap and sometimes boiling water. Test continuing. |
| Much faster drying than HBT. (Note: True only of poplin.) | Poplin far superior to HBT; this characteristic of first importance. |
| No comment. No mosquitoes at this time of year. | Excellent for all fabrics, including HBT. All uniforms impregnated with dimethyl phthalate. |
| Eliminate. | Eliminate. |
| No comment. | Eliminate. |
| Liked by some for added warmth (weather cool to cold). | Eliminate. |
| Satisfactory. | Add pencil slot; remove pleat. |
| Eliminate cuff gusset or redesign. | Simplify cuff closure. |
| No comment. | Shorten jacket one inch. |
| Liked. | No comment. |
| Use plastic buttons with thread eyes counter sunk. | Use strong sewn-on buttons. |

**(continued)**

## Theater Tests of the Tropical Uniform (continued)

| Test Period | 37th Inf. Div. (OQMG Test 293, Bougainville) Jul–Oct 44 | 7th Inf. Div. (OQMG Test 309A) Oct 44–Feb 45 |
|---|---|---|
| **11. Trouser design** | | |
| a. Suspender buttons | Eliminate. | Eliminate. |
| b. CWS fly | Eliminate. | No comment. |
| c. Watch pocket | No comment. | Retain. |
| d. Slash pockets | Retain. | Retain. |
| e. Cargo pockets | Eliminate. | Eliminate. |
| f. Hip pockets | Add at least one. | "Many want them." |
| g. Drawstring closure | Retain. | Retain. |
| h. Button type | See 10h. | See 10h. |
| **12. Sizing** | No comment. | Reduce sizing one size. |
| **13. Basis of issue** | No comment. | Theater recommends immediate standardization. Issue in place of all HBT in tropics, with priority given to infantry combat troops. |

*Note:

| **Official nomenclatures are as follows:** | **Terminology in this report:** |
|---|---|
| Cloth, Cotton, Wind Resistant, Poplin | Poplin |
| Cloth, Cotton, Wind Resistant, Byrd Cloth | Byrd Cloth |
| Cloth, Cotton, Wind Resistant, Oxford, 6.5 oz. | Oxford |
| Cloth, Cotton, Uniform Twill, 8.2 oz. | Uniform Twill |
| Cloth, Cotton, Herringbone Twill | HBT |
| Water Repellent Treatment | WRT |

**The khaki uniform consists of: Jacket, Cloth, Cotton, Uniform Twill, 6 oz. khaki
Trousers, Cloth, Cotton, Uniform Twill, 8.2 oz. khaki

| 124th Cavalry Regt. (Sp.) (OQMG Test 309B) Oct 44–Mar 45 | 41st Inf. Div. (OQMG Test 309C) May–Jun 44 |
|---|---|
| Eliminate. | Eliminate. |
| See 10c. | Eliminate. |
| No comment. | Retain. |
| Satisfactory. | Retain. |
| Location and design debatable. | Eliminate. |
| No comment. | Add two. |
| Retain. | Retain. |
| See 10h. | See 10h. |
| Many sleeves 1½″–2″ too long. 180/870 uniforms were too large to fit personnel. | Develop accurate tariff or use USAFFE tariff. |
| No comment. | Either 3 per individual or 2 per individual plus cotton khaki uniform.** |

# Quartermaster Board and Infantry Board Tests of Tropical Uniforms

| | Quartermaster Board (OQMG Test 1450, Florida) |
|---|---|
| 1. Garments tested | Jackets and trousers, poplin, WRT and non-WRT<br>Jackets and trousers, uniform twill<br>Jackets and trousers, Byrd cloth<br>Jackets and trousers, nylon-filled poplin<br>Jackets and trousers, nylon<br>Jackets and trousers, oxford |
| 2. Fabric | All closely woven lightweight fabrics preferred to HBT and uniform twill. Recommended (other than nylon): Byrd cloth, oxford. |
| 3. Durability | Satisfactory in forty-two-day test: Byrd cloth, oxford, poplin, HBT. |
| 4. Heat load | All closely woven, lightweight fabrics cooler than HBT and uniform twill. Included are poplin, WRT and non-WRT, Byrd cloth, oxford. |
| 5. Dirt penetration | No comment. |
| 6. Water absorption | WRT poplin absorbed less water than non-WRT poplin or oxford. All absorbed much less than HBT and uniform twill. No recommendation on WRT. |
| 7. Launderability | Shrinkage negligible in hand laundering and slight in mobile unit laundering. No comment on ease of washing. |
| 8. Drying time | Lightweight fabrics dry rapidly as compared with HBT and uniform twill. |

## Infantry Board
## (OQMG Test 293, Infantry Board, Ft. Benning, Ga.)

Jackets and trousers, poplin, WRT and non-WRT Trousers, uniform twill

WRT poplin recommended for jacket, uniform twill for trousers.

Uniform twill recommended for trousers; poplin OK for jackets.

No differences noted by measurement of sweat rate; all soldiers preferred poplin to HBT.

Mud and dirt can be brushed off poplin easily after the uniform dries.

WRT poplin the lightest uniform when exposed to rain and perspiration. Non-WRT poplin absorbs much less water than HBT or uniform twill. WRT recommended.

Shrinkage was slight in all fabrics. Poplin uniforms were easy to wash.

WRT poplin dried in half the time required for non-WRT poplin after both were submerged in water for one hour. Rate of drying proportional to water content.

**(continued)**

## QMB and Infantry Board Tests (continued)

| | Quartermaster Board (OQMG Test 1450, Florida) |
|---|---|
| **9. Mosquito protection** | Byrd cloth, oxford excellent; poplin good; uniform twill and HBT poor. |
| **10. Design of jacket** | |
| a. Shoulder loops | Retain. |
| b. Neck buttons | No comment. |
| c. CWS flap | Retain, but tack down. |
| d. Pockets | No comment except as noted in 11d. |
| e. Sleeve design | Replace with plain or raglan sleeves, with button-holed spun nylon drawstring in tunneled closure at wrists. |
| f. Jacket length | No comment. |
| g. Button type | No comment. |
| **11. Design of trousers** | |
| a. Suspender buttons | Replace by suspender buttonholes, placing buttons on suspenders. |
| b. CWS fly | Retain. |
| c. Crotch | No comment. |
| d. Watch pocket | Eliminate; add waterproof insert pocket inside left jacket pocket. |
| e. Slash pockets | Eliminate. |
| f. Cargo pockets | Retain but strengthen. |
| g. Hip pockets | Add right hip pocket. |
| h. Drawstring closure | Retain but use nylon drawstring. |
| i. Button type | No comment. |
| **12. Sizing** | All garments too large by one tariff size. |
| **13. Basis of issue** | No comment. |

## Infantry Board
## (OQMG Test 293, Infantry Board, Ft. Benning, Ga.)

Poplin and uniform twill excellent, HBT poor.

"Serve no purpose."
No comment.
No comment.
Jacket pockets were large enough.
Jacket cuffs are bulky.

No comment.
No comment.

Eliminate.

No comment.
Should be looser and reinforced.
No comment.

Retain.
Retain.
No comment.
Replace with flap and button.
No comment.

No comment.

No comment.

# Glossary

**A/B:** *Airborne*
**ABWD:** *Armored Board Winter Detachment*
**ANC:** *Army Nurse Corps*
**Arm:** *Armored*
**BAR:** *Browning Automatic Rifle*
**Bd:** *Board*
**Bn:** *Battalion*
**Cav:** *Cavalry*
**CBI:** *China-Burma-India*
**Div:** *Division*
**Engr:** *Engineer*
**ETO:** *European Theater of Operations*
**HBT:** *Herringbone Twill*
**Inf:** *Infantry*
**LST:** *Landing Ship Tank*
**M:** *Model**
**Mtn:** *Mountain*
**OQMG:** *Office of the Quartermaster General*
**OSS:** *Office of Strategic Studies*
**QMB:** *Quartermaster Board*
**SCR:** *Signal Corps Radio*
**SHAEF:** *Supreme Headquarters Allied Expeditionary Force*
**SWPA:** *Southwest Pacific Area*
**T:** *Test*
**USA:** *United States Army*
**V-E:** *Victory in Europe*
**WAAC:** *Women's Army Auxiliary Corps*
**WAC:** *Women's Army Corps*
**WAVES:** *Women Accepted for Volunteer Emergency Service*
**WD:** *War Department*

*Quartermaster items were sequenced by year as "Model of" until 1919, when "Model of" was officially abbreviated to "M," hence M1919. This form is used for consistency throughout this volume regardless of adoption date. The Ordnance Corps categorized items serially by "Model" (M1, M2, etc.) type instead of year.

# Sources

## Primary Quartermaster Files

The primary source documents researched for this work (except for the photographic material) were contained in National Archives Records Group 92, Office of the Quartermaster General (1940–1945), currently stored at the Suitland Reference Branch. Within this collection, most records actually utilized were found in the Quartermaster Research and Development (Decimal File 400.12) and Quartermaster Specifications for Manufacturing (Decimal File 400.11) files, both covering the period from 1926 through 1949.

## Official Works

Army Field Manual 21-15, War Department, Apr 45.

Army Regulations No. 600-35, War Department, 10 Nov 41 and 31 Mar 44 (with pertinent changes).

Army Regulations No. 600-36, War Department, 7 Feb 42 and 25 Feb 44 (with pertinent changes).

Army Regulations No. 600-37, War Department, 29 Jul 43 and 16 Apr 45 (with pertinent changes).

Army Regulations No. 600-40, War Department, 28 Aug 41 and 31 Mar 44 (with pertinent changes).

Army Regulations No. 600-90, War Department, 24 Feb 44 and 3 Feb 45 (with pertinent changes).

Army Regulations No. 615-40, War Department, 24 Apr 43 and 1 Feb 45 (with pertinent changes).

Dill, Dr. David B., *Textile, Clothing, and Footwear Division Clothing Branch Report No. 22: History of World War II Development of Jungle Warfare Uniform*, Quartermaster Research and Engineer Command, Jun 61.

*Medical Supply Catalog 6: List of Items for Troops, Posts, Camps, and Stations*, Headquarters, Army Service Forces, 1 Mar 44.

Pitkin, Thomas M., *Quartermaster Historical Series No. 5: Quartermaster Equipment for Special Forces*, Office of the Quartermaster General, 1944.

*Quartermaster Supply Catalog 3-1: List of Items for Troop Issue—Enlisted Men's Clothing and Equipment*, Headquarters, Army Service Forces, Aug 43 and May 46 (formerly issued as Quartermaster Supply Catalog, Section I, and OQMG Circular No. 4).

*Quartermaster Supply Catalog 3-2: List of Items for Troop Issue—WACS' and Nurses' Clothing and Equipment*, Headquarters, Army Service Forces, 1 Apr 44 and May 46 (formerly issued as Quartermaster Supply Catalog, Section II).

*Quartermaster Supply Catalog 3-3: List of Items for Issue to Posts, Camps, and Stations*, Headquarters, Army Service Forces, 15 Jun 44 (formerly issued as Quartermaster Supply Catalog, Section IV).

*Quartermaster Supply Catalog 3-4: List of Items for Issue to Troops, Miscellaneous Organizational Equipment*, Headquarters, Army Service Forces, 1945 (formerly issued as Quartermaster Supply Catalog, Section V).

*Quartermaster Supply Catalog 6: Chests, Kits, Outfits, and Sets*, Headquarters, Army Service Forces, 31 Jan 44 (formerly issued as Quartermaster Supply Catalog, Section IV).

Risch, Erna, *Quartermaster Historical Series No. 12: A Wardrobe for the Women of the Army*, Office of the Quartermaster General, 1945.

Risch, Erna, and Thomas Pitkin, *Quartermaster Historical Series No. 16: Clothing the Soldier of World War II*, Office of the Quartermaster General, 1946.

## Photograph Sources

*Key to position of photograph on page:* U–*upper*, M–*middle or second in sequence*, L–*lower*

**Adjutant General's Office (Army Staff Records Collection):** 7, 10U, 10M, 11–13, 14U, 16, 22, 23, 25, 28L, 40–42, 46U, 53U, 69–73, 79L, 98, 136L, 160, 176, 177, 182L, 190L, 191U, 198U, 200, 206U, 216–18, 226M, 229

**American Red Cross:** 191L

**Armored Board Winter Detachment P-473-4 Final Report (App.D):** 79U(D-123), 136M (D-111), 186U(D-180), 187U(D-177), 187M (D-178), 187L(D-112), 188U(D-113), 188M (D-109), 188L(D-131), 189U(D-110), 189M(D-115), 189L(D-114), 192U(D-128), 192M(D-129)

**Army Museums and Ordnance Bureau:** 4U, 5, 17U, 33U, 91

**Bachrach Photographic Studio:** 14L

**Chemical Corps (Edgewood Arsenal) Protective Division and Toxicological Research Library Photographic Collection:** 244L, 246, 247, 249

**Engineer Board, Office of the Chief of Engineers:** 99U, 106, 107

**National Archives Records of the Army Air Forces:** 31L, 39, 183M

**Office of the Army Surgeon General:** 77L, 223L, 227

**Office of the Quartermaster General:** 14L, 15, 49–51, 95–97, 102, 103, 105, 109L, 116, 124U, 125–27, 152U, 159L, 169, 170, 173–75, 178, 179, 201, 204, 205, 225U, 234L, 244U, 245, 253–55

**Quartermaster Board T-149 Final Report (Appendix Exhibits):** 110(I-C), 111U(XIII-F), 111L(XIII-G), 112–13(XIII-C), 114(XIII-F), 115(XIII-G), 117(XIII-E), 118(VII-D), 119U(VII-C), 119L(VII-E), 120–21(IV-F), 122–23(IV-C), 124L(VI-D)

**Quartermaster Board T-188 Final Report (Appendix Exhibits):** 219(A), 220(F), 221(G), 222U(H), 222M(I), 222L(I)

**Quartermaster Board T-250 Final Report (Appendix Exhibit L):** 250

**Quartermaster Board T-313 Final Report (Appendix Exhibit R):** 237L

**Quartermaster Board T-314 Final Report (Appendix Exhibits):** 224(L), 225M(K), 226U(H), 228(I), 230(A), 231U(N), 231M(O), 235U(Q), 235L(R), 236U(P), 236L(T), 238L(W)

**Quartermaster Board T-315 Final Report (Appendix Exhibits):** 223U(N), 225L(T), 232M(K), 232L(K), 233(L), 234U(L), 238U(Q)

**SHAEF D-Day Chemical Exhibit of Brig. Gen. Hugh Rowan:** 248

**U.S. Army Pacific Pictorial Archives:** 8L, 9, 44, 74–76, 148–50, 153L, 154, 155U, 157L, 158

**U.S. Army Signal Corps:** 3, 4U, 17L, 18, 20L, 21, 24, 26, 27, 28U, 31U, 33L, 34, 37U, 38, 43, 45, 46L, 52, 53L, 54–56, 58–61, 62L, 63–68, 77U, 78, 80, 92, 128–33, 135, 136U, 137, 139L, 140–47, 151U, 152L, 153U, 156, 157U, 157M,

161L, 162, 166, 167, 168L, 171, 172, 180U, 180L, 190U, 192L, 197L, 198L, 199, 208L, 209, 210, 213, 215L, 237U

**U.S. Army via Carter Rila:** 6, 8U, 10L, 19U, 35, 36, 47, 48, 100, 101, 104, 134, 138, 139U, 155L, 159U, 161U, 163L, 168U, 180M, 181, 182U, 183M, 183L, 195, 196, 232U, 243, 251

**U.S. Army via John Andrews:** 202, 203, 206L, 207, 208U

**U.S. Navy:** 151L

**War Department Office of War Information:** 19L, 20U, 29, 30, 32, 37L, 62U, 93, 94, 99L, 108, 109U, 163U, 184, 185, 186L, 197U, 214, 215U

# Index